Tribute to Henry A. "Hank" Rosso

THIS WORKBOOK SERIES is dedicated to the legacy of Henry A. "Hank" Rosso, noted by many experts as one of the leading figures in the development of organized philanthropic fund raising in the twentieth century. This series of workbooks, ranging from *Developing Your Case for Support* to *Building Your Endowment*, was the last project he undertook before his health failed him. The Indiana University Center on Philanthropy, of which he was a founder, is honored to have been asked to complete this project on Hank's behalf. My colleagues and I dedicate this series to his memory.

I am grateful to my colleague Tim Seiler for agreeing to serve as editor. Tim is director of The Fund Raising School, the national and international training program that Hank started in 1974. It is appropriate that this workbook series be tied directly to concepts and materials taught by The Fund Raising School.

By carefully studying the practitioners and scholars in fund raising who came before him, Hank was able to codify and teach principles and techniques for effective philanthropic fund raising. Scores of practitioners who applied his principles have been successful in diversifying their philanthropic fund raising and donor bases in sustaining their worthy causes. Hank was constantly concerned that those who might most need the information of The Fund Raising School might be least able to access it. He developed special courses for small organizations and edited *Achieving Excellence in Fund Raising* to get information into the hands of practitioners. This workbook series was for Hank another attempt to put the tools of effective philanthropic fund raising into the hands of practitioners who could not get to The Fund Raising School courses.

We hope you find this material useful to you in your work. One of Hank's favorite sayings was, "You can raise a lot more money with organized fund raising than you can with disorganized fund raising." We hope it helps you organize and find success in your fund raising activities. As you carry out your work, remember Hank's definition: "Fund raising is the gentle art of teaching the joy of giving."

Eugene R. Tempel
Executive Director
Indiana University Center on Philanthropy

FORTHCOMING BOOKS IN THE EXCELLENCE IN FUND RAISING WORKBOOK SERIES:

Building Your Endowment

Setting Up Your Annual Fund

EXCELLENCE IN FUND RAISING WORKBOOK SERIES TITLES AVAILABLE NOW:

Preparing Your Capital Campaign

Planning Special Events

Building Your Direct Mail Program

Developing Your Case for Support

THE JOSSEY-BASS NONPROFIT AND PUBLIC MANAGEMENT SERIES ALSO INCLUDES:

Achieving Excellence in Fund Raising, Henry A. Rosso and Associates

The Five Strategies for Fundraising Success, Mal Warwick

Conducting a Successful Capital Campaign, Second Edition, Kent E. Dove

Winning Grants Step by Step, Mim Carlson

The Fundraising Planner: A Working Model for Raising the Dollars You Need, Terry and Doug Schaff

The Jossey-Bass Guide to Strategic Communications for Nonprofits, Kathleen Bonk, Henry Griggs, Emily Tynes

Marketing Nonprofit Programs and Services, Douglas B. Herron

Transforming Fundraising: A Practical Guide to Evaluating and Strengthening Fundraising to Grow with Change, Judith E. Nichols

The Grantwriter's Start-Up Kit, Successful Images, Inc.

Secrets of Successful Grantsmanship, Susan L. Golden

How to Write Successful Fundraising Letters, Mal Warwick

The Excellence in Fund Raising Workbook Series

WORKBOOK SERIES

THE FUND RAISING WORKBOOK SERIES began with Hank Rosso and his vision of a set of separate yet interrelated workbooks designed to offer practical, high-quality models for successful fund raising. Each workbook focuses on a single topic and provides narrative material explaining the topic, worksheets, sample materials, and other practical advice. Designed and written for fund raising professionals, nonprofit leaders, and volunteers, the workbooks provide models and strategies for carrying out successful fund raising programs. The texts are based on the accumulated experience and wisdom of veteran fund raising professionals as validated by research, theory, and practice. Each workbook stands alone yet is part of a bigger whole. The workbooks are similar in format and design and use as their primary textual content the curriculum of The Fund Raising School as originally developed and written by Hank Rosso, Joe Mixer, and Lyle Cook. Hank selected or suggested authors for the series and intended to be coeditor of the series. The authors stay true to Hank's philosophy of fund raising, and the series is developed as a form of stewardship to Hank's ideals of ethical fund raising. All authors address how their contributions to the series act in tandem with the other steps in Hank's revolutionary Fund Raising Cycle, as illustrated here. It is the intent of the editor and of the publisher that this will be the premier hands-on workbook series for fund raisers and their volunteers.

Dedicated to the advancement of ethical fund raising

The Fund Raising School

Timothy L. Seiler
General Series Editor
Director, The Fund Raising School
Indiana University Center on Philanthropy

The Fund Raising Cycle

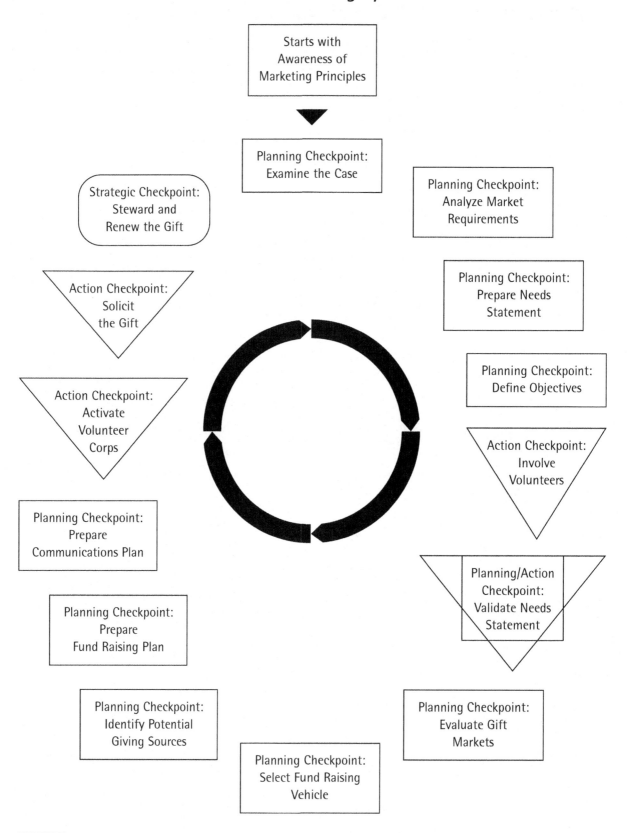

Starts with
Awareness of
Marketing Principles

Planning Checkpoint:
Examine the Case

Planning Checkpoint:
Analyze Market
Requirements

Strategic Checkpoint:
Steward and
Renew the Gift

Planning Checkpoint:
Prepare Needs
Statement

Action Checkpoint:
Solicit
the Gift

Planning Checkpoint:
Define Objectives

Action Checkpoint:
Activate
Volunteer
Corps

Action Checkpoint:
Involve
Volunteers

Planning Checkpoint:
Prepare
Communications Plan

Planning/Action
Checkpoint:
Validate Needs
Statement

Planning Checkpoint:
Prepare
Fund Raising Plan

Planning Checkpoint:
Identify Potential
Giving Sources

Planning Checkpoint:
Evaluate Gift
Markets

Planning Checkpoint:
Select Fund Raising
Vehicle

Source: Henry A. Rosso and Associates, *Achieving Excellence in Fund Raising,* p. 10. Copyright © 1991 Jossey-Bass Inc., Publishers. Reprinted by permission of Jossey-Bass Inc., a subsidiary of John Wiley & Sons, Inc.

PLANNING AND IMPLEMENTING YOUR MAJOR GIFTS CAMPAIGN

EXCELLENCE IN
FUND RAISING

WORKBOOK SERIES

Series Editor
Timothy L. Seiler

PLANNING AND IMPLEMENTING YOUR MAJOR GIFTS CAMPAIGN

SUZANNE IRWIN-WELLS

JOSSEY-BASS
A Wiley Company
www.josseybass.com

Published by

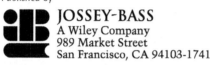

JOSSEY-BASS
A Wiley Company
989 Market Street
San Francisco, CA 94103-1741

www.josseybass.com

Jossey-Bass is a registered trademark of John Wiley & Sons, Inc.

The materials that appear in this book (except those for which reprint permission must be obtained from the primary sources) may be reproduced for educational/training activities. We do, however, require that the following statement appear on all reproductions:

This free permission is limited to the reproduction of material for educational/training events. Systematic or large-scale reproduction or distribution (more than one hundred copies per year)—or inclusion of items in publications for sale—may be done only with prior written permission. Also, reproduction on computer disk or by any other electronic means requires prior written permission. Requests to the Publisher for permission should be addressed to the Permissions Department, John Wiley & Sons, Inc., 605 Third Avenue, New York, NY 10158-0012, (212) 850-6011, fax (212) 850-6008, e-mail: permreq@wiley.com.

Jossey-Bass books and products are available through most bookstores. To contact Jossey-Bass directly, call (888) 378-2537, fax to (800) 605-2665, or visit our website at www.josseybass.com.

Substantial discounts on bulk quantities of Jossey-Bass books are available to corporations, professional associations, and other organizations. For details and discount information, contact the special sales department at Jossey-Bass.

We at Jossey-Bass strive to use the most environmentally sensitive paper stocks available to us. Our publications are printed on acid-free recycled stock whenever possible and our paper always meets or exceeds minimum GPO and EPA requirements.

Library of Congress Cataloging-in-Publication Data

Irwin-Wells, Suzanne, date.
   Planning and implementing your major gifts campaign / Suzanne
Irwin-Wells.—1st ed.
       p. cm.—(The Jossey-Bass nonprofit and public
management series)
   ISBN 0-7879-5708-9 (alk. paper)
   1. Fund raising.   I. Title.   II. Series.
   HV41.2 .I78 2002
658.15'224—dc21

2001006209

PB Printing   10 9 8 7 6 5 4 3 2 1   FIRST EDITION

The Jossey-Bass
Nonprofit and Public Management Series

Contents

Figures, Exhibits and Worksheets

Preface

FUND RAISING IS THE FUEL that helps power the nonprofit engine *in meeting its mission*. But it is only a means. It is not the end. The end refers to the mission of your nonprofit organization and how meeting that mission will improve the lives of people and the communities in which you live and work.

Why Donors Invest

Most donors love to give. But let's face the facts. Although contributed dollars pay your organization's expenses, no donor I have ever met in thirty-two years of nonprofit work really cares whether a nonprofit organization can buy new computers, pay the rent, or even pay the staff. What donors do passionately want you to do is to use their investments wisely and imaginatively to meet your mission, to solve the community problems, and meet the needs you and they both care about. Knowing these problems are solved and these needs are met is their return on their investment.

Broadly speaking, *fund raising* refers to the managed process through which organizations build relationships with donors and prospective donors to allow them to act on their values. *Values* are the tangible or intangible things that are important to individuals. People give to people representing organizations that are making the world a better place, specifically a place that more closely represents the values of the donors.

Donor values may simply be core values such as compassion, inclusiveness, or excellence. However, they may also be more specific, such as housing the homeless, promoting diversity in higher education, or fostering artistic excellence. Simply put, donors want to invest money in your organization so you can meet your mission.

The Importance of Major Gifts

One way for donors to make investments in your organization is through *major gifts*. Successful major gifts fund raising is especially important in today's nonprofit sector. First, demand for nonprofits' services is rising. Local, state, and federal agencies are looking to nonprofits to deliver services or programs they can no longer provide due to decreased government funding or lessened public commitment to using tax monies to provide those services. This places a greater fund raising burden on nonprofits because they need to expand their programs to serve more people.

At the same time, individual giving through direct gifts and bequests already totals around 85 percent or more of all giving. The number of individuals with wealth or disposable income in this country is growing much faster than the number of corporations or foundations that fund nonprofits. And more and more of these people are making enough money that they can contribute substantial charitable gifts. The increased need to underwrite expanded programs and services combined with the immense numbers of people who have the capacity to make major gifts means that community needs and opportunities to raise the funds to meet these needs are simultaneously present. For organizations ready to consider a major gifts campaign, now may be the time.

Planning and implementing a major gifts campaign may enable an organization to raise more money than it ever raised before, diversify its funding streams and decrease its dependency on grants and labor-intensive special events, acquire loyal donors who will continue to give year after year, upgrade donors from smaller to larger gifts, stabilize income received from individual donors, secure gifts in the most cost-effective way, identify future board members and other volunteer leaders, test the case of the organization and learn how well individuals understand the organization's mission, and establish the foundation and infrastructure for a future endowment or capital campaign.

Any organization that is serious about its growth and future stability should consider this important source of support. This workbook is designed to help nonprofits, especially small and medium-sized ones, diversify their funding base and build relationships with the millions of individuals who would, if properly cultivated, involved, and asked, make major gifts. The information it contains about what works best, what may occasionally work, and what almost never works reflects my thirty-two years of experience in the nonprofit sector, working mainly in development with small and medium-sized organizations and having been involved in many, many major gift campaigns with goals ranging from $25,000 to $15 million.

Overcoming Reluctance to Seek Major Gifts

Some nonprofit organizations hesitate to seek big gifts. Here are some common misperceptions that can prevent nonprofits from deciding to conduct a major gifts campaign:

We don't have any prospects. Most organizations that have individual donors have at least some who are able to make significantly larger gifts than they have been asked for.

We don't have any volunteers who will ask for large gifts. Many volunteers are willing to participate as long as they are properly trained and supported and, especially important, as long as they are enthusiastic about the purpose of the campaign and feel the dollar goal is realistic.

Our staff are too busy. It often takes less time to manage the solicitation of one hundred major donor prospects at $1,000 or more than it does to implement a large fund raising event or many other fund raising activities.

We are too small [or too grassroots]—only large organizations can raise big gifts. Size is not the most important factor. Most organizations with strong missions, appealing cases, and well-thought-out plans can raise major gifts.

We don't have enough money in our budget to pay for a major gifts campaign. Major gifts campaigns are more cost effective than any other fund raising effort; expenses often range from only 5 to 15 percent of revenues whereas special events and direct-mail campaigns may cost more than they bring in.

We're in a financial crunch and need income urgently. Soliciting major gift prospects can be the best way to secure immediate funds and avoid future cash flow problems.

We won't succeed. Realistic goal setting will contribute to enthusiastic staff and volunteers and a successful campaign.

The Audience for This Book

Although almost every nonprofit can benefit from soliciting major gifts, this workbook was created especially to assist small and medium-sized organizations as they plan and implement their first major gifts campaign, increase the effectiveness of a current campaign, or jump-start a stalled campaign.

It offers guidance to both paid and volunteer staff who are novices or only moderately experienced at major gifts fund raising: executive directors of smaller organizations, who may be both chief executive and development director; annual fund directors thinking of mounting their first major gifts campaigns; development directors seeking to organize their nonprofits' successful but informal solicitation of major gifts; major gifts officers relatively new to their roles; members of boards of directors or volunteers with organizations with limited paid staff; and others in almost any small to medium-sized organization that seeks to stabilize contributed income, diversify funding sources, and decrease dependence on grants. All these people have a vested interest in a strong nonprofit organization that has sufficient funds to meet its mission. Successful major gifts campaigns can help organizations develop this strength.

How to Use This Book

This workbook is different from most fund raising books in that it is short on philosophy and long on worksheets. That is because my goal is to assist you in planning and managing an actual, effective major gifts campaign, using this workbook and its worksheets as your guide. If your organization is one of the many smaller organizations with very limited development budgets, this workbook can be your personal fund raising consultant. Let it be your hands-on guide as you develop the worksheets that outline your campaign and as you, step-by-step, implement and monitor a successful effort. Later, you can use the workbook and the worksheets you completed the first time you used them as a personal journal that you can review when you plan your next major gifts campaign.

The workbook format means that you can read the materials in a relatively short amount of time. The worksheets encourage you to respond immediately to the ideas you have just read about, applying them directly to your own situation and information. I also suggest that the first time you use this workbook, you go through all the chapters in order so as not to miss any critical steps. Even if you are more experienced in fund raising, you might find Chapter One, "Understanding Major Gifts," a useful review.

Of course, because of this book's brevity, you won't find every idea there is on major gifts campaigns. For further information and guidance, I suggest you check out some of the outstanding books listed in the back.

Completing this workbook can help you strengthen your organization's ability to meet its mission by increasing support, engaging volunteers in meaningful and productive ways, and diversifying the funding base. It can assist you in giving your staff and volunteers the confidence to plan and implement a successful major gifts campaign and in helping them overcome objections to starting one. And as your expertise grows from the many real-life examples and practical exercises, it can increase your chances of meeting your campaign goals.

The Example Set by Hank Rosso

This workbook is in many ways a tribute to Hank Rosso's dedication to fund raising excellence. I first met Henry A. Rosso in the mid-1970s, when I was a volunteer working on a fledgling campaign for a small, struggling women's organization. At the time I was afraid to ask people for money because I thought I would fail and let everybody down. And I was sure major gifts campaigning was an activity I could never master. But Hank told me, "Let your passion for your mission do the talking and the rest will follow."

To me, Hank was the embodiment of the nonprofit sector—a positive voice that led people to get involved, to change the things that are wrong and preserve the things that are right. I think Hank was most helpful to me when he made fund raising seem so basic and doable in a step-by-step way. He cut through the jargon and my can't-do attitude to get to the core—that major gifts fund raising can be a manageable process for most organizations. People who never met Hank can still hear his voice in his extremely helpful book *Achieving Excellence in Fund Raising*.

When I look back over my thirty-two years of work in the nonprofit sector and see how little I knew when I started and how much I have learned since, thanks to Hank and many other wonderful teachers, I realize how important it is to believe in *yourself*. Fund raising inevitably involves taking risks and trying new things. Sometimes the fear of taking these risks can prevent you from trying. I believe that instilling confidence in others is the single most important thing a consultant or teacher can do. Hank Rosso was the all-time expert.

Acknowledgments

I want to recognize the millions of people who work with, volunteer with, or support nonprofit organizations. You help make our world a more wonderful place.

And I would also like to thank my nearest and dearest—Geanene, Victoria, Ashley, Karen, and Frankie.

Mill Valley, California   Suzanne Irwin-Wells
October 2001

Dedicated to
Henry A. "Hank" Rosso
(1918–1999)
An enchanting teacher
who loved his students and
the sector in which they worked

The Author

SUZANNE IRWIN-WELLS is founder and principal of Irwin-Wells Associates, a California-based fund raising consulting firm serving philanthropic organizations in the United States and the United Kingdom. She has worked with nonprofits since 1969, serving as both development director and consultant. In addition to serving as a consultant, she is adjunct professor at Golden Gate University in San Francisco, where she teaches fund raising. Her alma maters include Northwestern University, Golden Gate University, and the University of San Francisco. She has served on numerous boards and has co-founded several organizations.

PLANNING AND IMPLEMENTING YOUR MAJOR GIFTS CAMPAIGN

CHAPTER 1

Understanding Major Gifts

MAJOR GIFTS FUND RAISING is interrelated with other methods of fund raising and with other areas and functions of your organization such as finance and programs. This chapter offers an overview of fund raising so you can understand these interrelationships and the organizational context in which major gifts fund raising takes place. It also defines major gifts and describes how major gifts fund raising is often incorporated into an organization's development plan.

Major Gifts and the Fund Raising Cycle

Think of your organization and its mission as a vehicle. Fund raising is like a one hundred–spoke wheel that is constantly turning, and as it turns it moves that vehicle forward. Each spoke represents a different fund raising activity such as volunteer recruitment, prospect research, and solicitation. Fund raising is not done only during a certain time of each fiscal year or in a financial crisis—it is done all year long, year after year. It is a complex undertaking that requires discipline, planning, and preparation.

Look at the diagram of the Fund Raising Cycle at the front of this workbook. As you can see, a great deal of preparation is required before your organization is ready to solicit major gifts. It must first examine its case, prepare a needs assessment, identify objectives, involve volunteers, identify prospects, and create a fund raising plan.

Only after all these intensive, time-consuming activities is your organization ready for the action many people fear the most—solicitation. However, if you have carefully completed all the previous steps in the Fund Raising Cycle, you and your volunteers should be well prepared, and therefore sufficiently confident, to present your case to prospects. Clearly, the best fund raising plan in the world amounts to nothing unless someone is willing to ask for a gift. Fund raising, moreover, does not stop with solicitation, which represents only one spoke of the one-hundred-spoke wheel. When a gift is received, it must be properly acknowledged, with the understanding that your organization will be a wise steward of its use.

At this point, your organization begins planning to renew the gift, and it begins the cycle all over. (For more about the Fund Raising Cycle, read *Achieving Excellence in Fund Raising*, Rosso, 1991.)

The Donor Pyramid

If you have been doing fund raising for any length of time at all, you probably already know that the search for funds involves many sizes of gifts, many sources of gifts, and many vehicles through which they are secured. Direct mail is a vehicle that is often used to secure smaller gifts from many individuals. Face-to-face solicitation is a vehicle typically used to secure larger gifts from individuals. Planned giving is a vehicle that secures bequests from wills. It can result in large gifts that represent the transfer of accumulated assets like shares in a corporation or real estate from the donor to the nonprofit organization.

Through these various vehicles, successful fund raising programs typically bring individual donors up through the ranks of the organization's development or fund raising program, soliciting first smaller and eventually larger gifts, as illustrated in the donor pyramid (Figure 1.1), which is a concept popularized by Robert Blum and now widely used in the field.

The donor universe, the base of the pyramid, is the largest group and includes everyone who could conceivably support the organization. From this huge pool, you will select a much smaller number of individuals who will be asked to give; these prospective donors have characteristics that make them more likely than the others to give. An even smaller number will actually make gifts. The organization then seeks a renewal gift from those acquired donors, and succeeds in upgrading some of its retained donors to a larger gift amount. Among these donors and through other sources, you can identify major gifts prospects. Those who become major gift donors also become the prospects for your future capital or endowment campaigns. Only a very small number of your donors will make planned gifts. Some of these planned gift donors may have made major gifts before, but it is likely that many of them will never have made a major gift before.

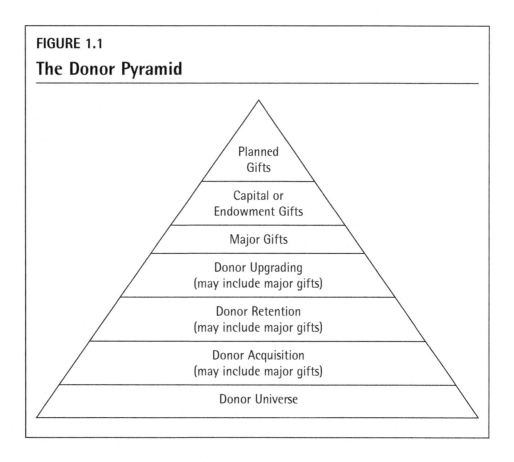

FIGURE 1.1

The Donor Pyramid

Planned Gifts

Capital or Endowment Gifts

Major Gifts

Donor Upgrading (may include major gifts)

Donor Retention (may include major gifts)

Donor Acquisition (may include major gifts)

Donor Universe

The Characteristics of Major Gifts

I have never heard of a nonprofit organization that gets gifts of the same size from all its donors. You will always find that some people give more than others. This is due to both level of interest and capacity to give. A major gift generally has these characteristics:

- It is large relative to the majority of gifts to the organization.
- It often evolves over what may be a lengthy period of time as a relationship with the prospect is cultivated.
- It is often solicited face-to-face, by one or two volunteers or by a volunteer and a member of the staff.
- It may be paid immediately or pledged and paid over time and may consist of appreciated assets (such as stock or real estate) as well as cash.

Different organizations will define major gifts differently. For a large university a major gift may be $25,000 and up. For a smaller arts or social service organization it may begin at $1,000 or even $250. In addition, keep in mind that organizations and donors may define major gifts differently. In the donors' eyes, all their gifts may be major ones.

Where Major Gifts Fit in an Integrated Development Plan

Your organization's mission concerns meeting external community needs in the local area or in a broader sphere. However, your organization also has its own internal needs. It has to meet these needs in order to focus on its external goals. An integrated organizational development plan employs different fund raising efforts for different needs.

One primary set of internal needs centers on ongoing operations and programs that have definite and fairly predictable expenses (the annual operating budget). These expenses must be met year after year. Your donors are willing to contribute toward these costs only because their gifts will enable your organization to solve the community problems and meet the community needs that are at the heart of your mission. Just as these expenses recur every year, so must the gifts that support them. No matter what else your organization is doing, it must support its operating expenses. These gifts are typically raised through the annual fund effort.

Once you acquire a base of donors who continue to give to your nonprofit's operating budget through contributions to the annual fund, you can raise their sights by inviting them to invest in something new or special. You might offer them a unique opportunity to support the expansion of a summer program for at-risk children, for example, or request their help in meeting a challenge grant for remodeling a learning center. Usually donors' gifts to special purpose campaigns are larger than their annual fund contributions. It is of course important to position these special purpose gifts as contributions in addition to and not instead of their annual fund gifts.

Occasionally your organization will have capital needs. These are often tangible things like new or renovated buildings, or the establishment or increase of an endowment fund, or the creation or expansion of a major program. Large gifts to capital campaigns are often paid over a multiyear period and may come from the donors' appreciated assets or investments. The best donors for these occasionally occurring capital needs are of course those very same donors who are already excited by your organization and who have invested in its mission.

The ultimate gifts are planned gifts. They may be given toward any of the needs described here. The term does not mean that donors do not plan other kinds of gifts. Rather, it means that a planned gift usually takes into account the donor's long-term investment strategies or estate plan and may involve the donor's financial adviser.

All four fund raising methods—annual, special purpose, capital, and planned—are part of an integrated development plan. In a successful plan, each method interacts well with the others. For example, let's say your organization is a library. You can't solicit special purpose gifts to expand your Spanish-language collection if you don't have a healthy annual fund that allows your organization to maintain the reading room and pay the librarian. The same holds true for soliciting capital and planned gifts. Donors will generally tell you to get your existing house in order before they will have the confidence to invest in any expansion plans.

Worksheet 1.1 will help you begin to understand your own organization's fund raising pattern as you create an overview of the numbers and sizes of gifts your organization has received for a recent twelve-month period and of the vehicles that brought these gifts in. Knowing what you are already doing to acquire gifts at different levels will help you determine the best strategies for a future major gifts campaign.

Major gifts are likely to be a part of each of the four integrated methods of fund raising. Your annual fund will probably include some major gifts. It is to be hoped that your special purpose efforts will also include several large gifts. And the foundation of all capital and endowment efforts will be major gifts. And of course major gifts may also be sought through programs or campaigns designed especially for that purpose. The remainder of this chapter will discuss ongoing major gifts efforts and introduce the focus of this workbook, the major gifts campaign and the way people must work together to make that campaign a success.

Ongoing Major Gifts Efforts

An ongoing major gifts effort may be part of an annual giving program or a separate program with its own staff.

Major Gifts and the Annual Fund

Because people have different capacities to give and differing levels of commitment to organizations, it is understandable that every annual giving program will bring in gifts of various amounts. The experience of most nonprofits is that 10 to 20 percent of donors give 60 to 80 percent of the funds raised in any one year or any one effort. These top-level donors are among the ones who are called major gift donors. The most effective annual giving programs will identify the donors who have the capacity to give at a selected high level and will treat them differently by personalizing their mail and asking to meet with them to discuss their gifts face-to-face.

An organization may set a major gifts goal for its annual giving program. This kind of major gift fund raising is often sufficient if the purpose is for ongoing programs. Often major gifts made through the annual fund program are unrestricted.

WORKSHEET 1.1

Assessing Your Current Gift Program

Select a twelve-month time period to examine, and then complete this chart of gifts to your organization during that period. Use any resources you need. The more accurate the figures, the more useful this activity will be to you.

Time period: _____

Gift Vehicle	Number of Gifts $0– $99	Number of Gifts $100– $499	Number of Gifts $500– $999	Number of Gifts $1,000– $4,999	Number of Gifts $5,000– $9,999	Number of Gifts $10,000 and Over	Total $$
Direct mail	_____	_____	_____	_____	_____	_____	_____
Special events	_____	_____	_____	_____	_____	_____	_____
Web site	_____	_____	_____	_____	_____	_____	_____
Face-to-face	_____	_____	_____	_____	_____	_____	_____
Grants	_____	_____	_____	_____	_____	_____	_____
Planned gifts	_____	_____	_____	_____	_____	_____	_____
Capital campaign	_____	_____	_____	_____	_____	_____	_____
Endowment campaign	_____	_____	_____	_____	_____	_____	_____
Other	_____	_____	_____	_____	_____	_____	_____
Total	_____	_____	_____	_____	_____	_____	_____

Incorporating major gifts into your annual campaign may have the following benefits. It can help institutionalize major gifts fund raising, making it an automatic part of your development planning year after year. It can help you leverage bigger gifts from smaller givers and raise total giving. For example, if you show smaller givers that $50,000 toward a $100,000 major gifts goal has already been secured from ten donors, it gives them the feeling they are supporting an effort likely to reach its goal and also encourages them to think bigger. Moreover, an annual campaign that incorporates major gifts may not require board approval or may be easier to get board approval for than a separate major gifts campaign would be. Finally, seeking major gifts during your annual campaign does not preclude conducting a separate campaign for major gifts. Some organizations, for instance, seek major gifts during every annual giving effort and also conduct separate major gifts campaigns to fund special community needs.

There are also some drawbacks to including major gifts in your annual campaign. People may assume this takes the place of an organized campaign for a special need and may hesitate to see the need or opportunity for a separate major gifts campaign. Donors may hesitate to give as much as they can to the annual effort because it may not seem as important as a separate campaign. It may be hard to get donors to make "stretch gifts" that are paid over time if they believe that the organization may begin expecting them to make similar gifts annually.

The Ongoing Major Gifts Program

A major gifts program is a recurring effort to identify, cultivate, and solicit major gift prospects who may make large gifts for both unrestricted and restricted uses. Such a program happens year after year. If your development staff and organization are large enough, you may have a staff person, a major gifts officer or director, dedicated to this effort. Generally organizations that have a special major gifts program will also raise major gifts through their annual giving effort.

The Major Gifts Campaign

Although all effective fund raising programs should establish long-term major gifts strategies, this workbook is designed to help readers on a more time- and goal-oriented level: the establishment and implementation of a major gifts campaign. A major gifts campaign is different from an ongoing major gifts program in three key ways. First, it more likely has a specific fund raising goal. Second, the organization's volunteers participate intensively. Third, the campaign is time limited, with specific start and finish dates. (This last characteristic is one of the reasons volunteers may be willing to solicit major gifts during a campaign. They know they are not committing themselves to a never-ending effort.) Although major gifts raised through a major gifts program *may* be restricted to a special use, a time-specific campaign is *typically* conducted for a nonrecurring and specific purpose.

If your organization currently receives major gifts through an annual fund effort or a donor acquisition mailing or just "over the transom," that does not necessarily mean it is ready for or even needs a structured major gifts campaign. You must also consider whether the organization has a compelling special need that a campaign conducted over a limited time might satisfy.

Here are some of the most important resources you will need for a successful major gifts campaign:

- Adequate donor prospects to meet your goal. You will learn more about this in Chapter Four.

- One or more people who can provide support services, such as mailing out packets to solicitors, updating donor records, coordinating events, and preparing campaign reports.

- A budget for materials, brochures, training, cultivation events, and donor recognition and stewardship. You will learn more about this in Chapter Five.

- Someone to provide ongoing and enthusiastic leadership to the campaign volunteers and staff. You will learn more about volunteers and how to lead them in Chapter Six.

- Someone with the experience and expertise to train volunteers in face-to-face solicitation or other fund raising techniques.

- A well thought out, inspirational, clear, and believable campaign prospectus.

- A well-conceived plan with clearly stated tasks and timelines showing who is responsible for each task. You will learn more about this in Chapter Ten.

- A recognition plan to acknowledge gifts and recognize donors. You will learn more about this in Chapter Eleven.

- A stewardship plan to involve the donors after the campaign ends.

Working Together to Solicit Major Gifts

Planning and managing the annual campaign, soliciting special purpose gifts, meeting capital and endowment goals, and running a major gifts campaign takes a lot of work and effort. Fund raising is increasingly a complex undertaking that requires careful planning and goal setting and in which many different people play important and interrelated roles.

In some organizations, there are clear delineations among different kinds of fund raising. A medium-sized organization may have a four-person development department with a development director, database manager and donor relations assistant, annual fund director, and administrative assistant. Small organizations may have one-person development shops, with one individual doing all the fund raising. In even smaller or new organizations, the executive director may also be the only fund raiser.

To be most successful, major gifts fund raising in particular must be a shared responsibility. I like to think that gone are the days when nonprofit boards said to key staff, "Go after major gifts, and let us know how it goes." Nowadays, many staff members and also volunteers from board members on down have important roles in major gifts campaigns.

Good ongoing communication between the development and finance offices is critical. It usually doesn't matter which office processes the gifts as long as both groups talk to each other and there is a mutually agreed upon, written gift recording, acknowledgment, and reporting process. Ideally the development office should have easy access to the finance office and vice versa as part of ensuring the accurate records every fund raiser relies on.

Because your program staff and your volunteer coordinators may encounter potential contributors on a daily basis and even know some of them well, routine communication across the organization is the key to a successful effort. Worksheet 1.2 will help you with your communication.

Here are some easy ways to involve busy, over-worked program staff in your campaign:

Involve key people in the planning process. If you're a major gifts director and you want the cooperation of annual fund directors, ask them to participate in shaping the major gifts campaign.

Be sure your supervisors are on board and well informed. Their support and understanding are essential.

Communicate campaign goals at staff meetings. Ideally, your organization holds regular meetings of key staff leaders—such as program coordinators, annual fund directors, database managers, and so on—at which you can emphasize fund raising goals and participants can exchange useful information. Such meetings, and even informal daily conversations, can also identify potential problems and act to prevent them from materializing.

Make sure everyone knows the campaign purpose. Tell everyone what the organization will be able to do when the campaign meets its dollar goals. Be sure to relate these goals to your mission. Is the $5,000 raised through the campaign earmarked for expansion of the after-school program? Will your organization be able to hire an additional part-time recreational therapist? Will your library be able to expand its collection of African American literature?

Encourage ongoing communication. Tell people you will maintain all confidentialities when they provide you with information about volunteers or participants they believe may be prospective donors. Then honor these confidences.

Share. Share. Share. Share both information and credit. A good campaign is one in which all the players win.

WORKSHEET 1.2

Identifying Staff and Volunteers Involved with Prospects

Use this worksheet to see your fund raising in a more comprehensive way, identify the players in your major gifts fund raising efforts, and understand whom to involve in your campaign. Use the additional spaces to list other people important to major gifts fund raising in your organization. Share the results with the key campaign participants to ensure they understand their own and others' roles.

Staff or Volunteer Title   **Involvement with Major Gifts**

Executive director _____

Major gifts director _____

Development director _____

Annual fund director _____

Special events director _____

Others (specify) _____

_____

_____

_____

A REAL-LIFE STORY OF MISSED OPPORTUNITIES

Leaders of an organization with a budget of about $4 million believed they were too dependent on government grants. They had a rudimentary development program and were beginning to think about major gifts. At the same time, however, because of impending budget cuts and possible layoffs, the executive director had cancelled the monthly all-staff meetings, and the fact that the agency was trying to raise funds from other sources was not passed on to all the staff.

One person who did not know the agency's plans was the program coordinator of the agency's training center for disabled adults. The coordinator had developed a relationship with an elderly woman whose husband had attended the center's programs daily, usually driven by his wife. After he died, his widow continued to visit the center, working as a volunteer. Over time she confided in the program coordinator that she had no close friends or relatives still living and that her estate, while not huge, nevertheless included valuable real estate and a nest egg of investments. Most important, she passionately wanted to honor her husband with some kind of memorial.

This information about the widow's personal values and desires to honor her husband never found its way to the development department. The widow died a year later, without a will. Given that the widow had no living relatives and no will, her estate likely passed to the government.

A REAL-LIFE STORY WITH A HAPPY ENDING

A very wealthy man, let's call him Mr. Livingston, who was not known as especially generous, became acquainted with Peter, the young program assistant of an organization that provides recreational and sports activities for children. Because they were both enthusiastic ice hockey fans, Mr. Livingston began inviting the young assistant to join him in his box seats at the home games. Peter knew from seeing Mr. Livingston's car that he was probably very wealthy. Then he saw Mr. Livingston mentioned in a newspaper article listing the wealthiest local residents. His name was near the top of the list, and he had a net worth of several hundred million dollars. Peter then spoke of Mr. Livingston to the development director of his organization at their next all-staff meeting. The development director followed through. About a year after Mr. Livingston and Peter first met, the organization received notification that Mr. Livingston was going to give it several million dollars to establish an endowment.

The core information I have presented here about fund raising and major gifts can help you understand where your organization is today in its fund raising program and how well it integrates some key concepts in successful fund raising. Understanding today is usually key to creating a successful tomorrow.

CHAPTER 2

Preparing for Major Gifts

NOW THAT YOU ARE well versed in the basics of major gifts, you are set to get ready for your major gifts campaign. In this chapter you will learn the essentials of developing a case statement, the role of the campaign manager, the importance of clear and ongoing communication, and the critical role of your database in managing your prospects and monitoring your efforts.

Fostering a Philanthropic Attitude

Before considering specific preparations, let's consider a basic preparation for a major gifts campaign. It has to do with the environment in which the campaign takes place. Perhaps the most important part of ensuring an ongoing successful major gifts effort is engendering a *philanthropic attitude* throughout your organization. This means:

- You are *educating* all your staff about the ways their work enables the organization to meet its mission. Each and every person is an important member of your team.

- You are keeping board members and other volunteers updated not only with the campaign goal but with success stories about *how their work is helping* the community.

- You are building *personal relationships* with your volunteers. You know them by their first names, and you always remember to greet them and thank them.

- You are finding formal and informal opportunities to speak to your donors at times other than when you are asking them for money. For example, you have thank-a-thons to call them for the sole purpose of saying, *"Thanks!"*

- You are always paying attention to your donors and volunteers and *listening* and *hearing* what they are saying. They sometimes see important things you do not because you are too busy or too close to an issue.

Remember, major gifts can increase the ongoing financial stability of your organization and significantly strengthen your ability to meet your mission. A *philanthropic attitude* costs nothing but can bring rich dividends to the people you serve. For more information about other key concepts of major gifts, refer to *Beyond Fund Raising* (Grace, 1999).

Developing a Case for Support

Your organization's case for support tells people your organization's cause. It articulates the justifications for supporting your organization as it advances its mission. Your organization's case statement is a key internal document that leads to case expressions, such as campaign case statements and brochures, grant proposals, and direct-mail letters. The case statement also has many uses inside the organization. It is used to educate staff so everyone, not just development staff, understands the importance of successful fund raising. It is used to orient new board members. It is used to recruit volunteers to the campaign.

Simply put, your case presents a community problem or need and tells why your organization is well poised to address this problem, how it plans to do so, what difference this will make to the prospective donors, and why they should support your organization's cause. (Notice how this follows the Fund Raising Cycle discussed in Chapter One.)

The case is such an essential document, you might think every organization has one. However, in my experience, most small to medium-sized organizations do not have such a document, although staff are often able to articulate the basic concepts of the organization's case. They have just never gotten around to developing the actual document. Many large organizations do not have case statement documents either. This means not only that they may not present the strongest case they could to their donors every time but that they are unprepared to respond quickly to funding opportunities. Some organizations have learned the hard way that you don't ever want to be caught without your case.

Like many things in fund raising, developing the case statement should never be done in isolation. Too often, development directors take on or are asked to take on case development all on their own. If an organization has a development director, that individual is usually the one who *begins* the process. When there is no development director, the executive director usu-

A REAL-LIFE STORY OF MISSED OPPORTUNITY

A prominent organization in a medium-sized town serving developmentally disabled children was successful in winning foundation grants because of the dynamic leadership of the executive director and the success stories of the children served. This overworked executive knew he should have a case statement. In fact it had been on his to-do list for over two years when the call came in from one of the wealthiest philanthropists in town. "What would you do if next week I gave you a million dollars?" this prospective donor asked. Taken aback, the executive director didn't know what to say. The donor asked him to send him the agency's case statement. Six months later the executive director still had not contacted the donor.

A REAL-LIFE STORY WITH A HAPPY ENDING

At a very small agency that serves undocumented U.S. residents, a woman unknown to the organization called the development director and said she had a windfall she wanted to give away although she would not say the amount. She had spoken to a few other groups and had told them, "Whoever gets material to me the quickest gets the gift."

The development director quickly and passionately told the caller the case: "We value all people in our community, no matter what circumstances brought them here. If we don't provide services to non-English-speaking people, they may never be able to get good jobs and earn a living to support their families. Our English language classes and job training workshops help people stand on their own feet." He added, "If we received a large gift, we would like to expand our peer-training program for the building trades. If you have a fax number or an e-mail address, I can get you a copy of our case statement right now. In English, Spanish, or Tagalog." The agency got the gift—the largest it has ever received—$150,000, over 50 percent of its annual budget. By the way, a copy of the multilingual case is included in the introductory packet the agency gives its clients, titled "Welcome to America."

ally initiates the case statement. In either case, the work begins by collecting case resources, information about the organization, such as its mission statement, goals, objectives, programs and services, governance, staffing, service delivery and facilities, planning and evaluation, and history. Supporting letters, testimonials and other quotations, lists of accomplishments, and so forth are also gathered. This process typically requires considerable cooperation from others.

After the person with primary responsibility for the case statement collects the resources, his or her next step is to draft the document. The draft is then typically forwarded, first, to the executive director, then to the board's development committee, then to the board, and finally to a sampling of the donors and potential donors. At each step, the case may be critiqued, refined, and edited. Worksheets 2.1 and 2.2 begin the process.

Developing Your Case

To practice articulating your case briefly and succinctly, pretend you have just received a call from a prospective donor who wants to give away a windfall. Take no more than ten minutes to write out your case, answering the questions as concisely as you can.

Why does our organization exist? What cause does it serve? What does it value?

Why should people care about what our organization does?

What difference does our organization make for our community?

How will a donor benefit?

Be sure to involve volunteers in this process as well. Remember, volunteers are advocates for your organization's cause and the ones who will solicit many of the prospective donors. Their involvement in case development educates them, teaching them ways to express the case to others, and it can increase their enthusiasm and commitment to your cause. Ultimately, once the case document is finalized, the board endorses it.

It is useful to formally chart your course as you begin to gather the resource materials to develop your case statement document, so you can identify missing parts promptly and give others early notice about what you need from them.

WORKSHEET 2.2

Finding the Pieces

Prepare to create your organization's case by charting the necessary resources.

Resource	Who Has It?	When, How, and by Whom Was It Developed?	If It Doesn't Exist, Who Should Create It?
Vision statement	_____	_____	_____
Values-based mission statement	_____	_____	_____
Goals	_____	_____	_____
Objectives	_____	_____	_____
Programs and services	_____	_____	_____
Governance	_____	_____	_____
Staffing	_____	_____	_____
Facilities, service delivery	_____	_____	_____
Finances	_____	_____	_____
Planning, evaluation	_____	_____	_____
History	_____	_____	_____
Supporting materials (specify)	_____	_____	_____

How long should the case statement be? It depends. If your organization has a long history and offers many distinct programs or services, its case statement might well be longer than that of a newer and less diversified group. If you believe length will be an issue for some readers, you can always write two versions—a brief one and a longer, more detailed one. I have seen well-written and compelling case statements that were a few pages long. And I have seen great ones that were thirty or more pages. Just keep in mind that you want people to read the case statement and that most people are busy. So brevity and clarity are important. Ultimately, you will probably want to go further and have different versions of your case statement for individuals, corporations, and foundations. Just remember, you're not alone in this process. Involve others. Your organization will benefit.

Developing the Campaign Case

The campaign case, or prospectus, for a major gifts campaign is an *expression* of your organization's case statement. The campaign case focuses on the needs addressed in the campaign goal. For example, if an arts organization currently serves public school children K–4 and seeks to increase its reach to serve children in grades 5 to 7, the campaign case explains why meeting that expanded need is important, how the organization plans to meet the need, and so on. The case expression will likely detail successes of the current program, in order to instill confidence in the institutional capacity for growth, and then proceed to describe the new program.

Being able to articulate the campaign case is essential for everyone in your organization and your campaign. Start with a brief case that can be the basis for a more detailed case with supporting documentation such as budgets, resumes of program directors, and the like. Complete Worksheet 2.3 yourself and also copy it for campaign staff and volunteers to fill out, as a way of getting their input. This exercise can also increase their sense of ownership of the campaign and make them more effective solicitors. (For more information about case development, see Timothy Seiler, *Developing Your Case for Support*, 2001.)

Fulfilling the Role of Campaign Manager

Earlier I assured you that the complex process of fund raising is not done by one individual. Now that you have begun the major gifts campaign process, you need to identify a campaign manager and to assign key responsibilities. This manager may be you. Certainly if your title is major gifts officer, you

WORKSHEET 2.3

Developing the Campaign Case Expression

Write a brief case (one hundred to two hundred words) for your major gifts campaign by answering the following questions.

For what purpose will funds raised from this campaign be used?

What community need does this purpose meet?

What happens if this need is not met?

What benefits result from meeting this need?

Why is our organization the best one to do this?

Why should the prospective donor care?

How does the donor benefit?

are the person most likely to manage this campaign. The next most likely choice might be the development director (again this might be you). If your organization is small and has no development staff, possibly the executive director will direct the campaign.

Now is the time to remember one of the commandments of campaign management: thou shalt not place a new, time-consuming responsibility on the shoulders of someone who already has a full-time job. It just won't work. This means your organization may have to hire additional staff. But it does not mean the new staff person has to be a professional campaign manager, as this case history illustrates.

A SMART MOVE IN CAMPAIGN HIRING

A medium-sized animal shelter serving a low-income neighborhood was turning away injured pets because its free clinic had only one part-time vet. The staff were confident they had enough potential donors to contribute the entire $150,000 to hire more staff and upgrade the treatment rooms, but they did not know who had time to plan and implement the campaign. The executive director considered hiring a campaign manager because the shelter's development director was already overburdened with work. But in the shelter's largely rural area, the executive director did not know where to find a qualified person. At the same time, the development director was eager to do a major gifts campaign as she had never had the experience and wanted to learn new things. The problem was resolved when the board allocated enough money to hire a full-time development assistant. That enabled the development director to take on this exciting new responsibility.

If you are the campaign's manager, no matter what your actual title, you have a vital role. Campaign management is basically people management because that is what your organization is—a group of people who have come together for a common purpose. Of course much that follows in this workbook applies to this role. Let's start here with a few basic and essential practices. Always remember to:

- Respect everyone involved. It's hard to meet your mission if you alienate those most closely involved.

- Communicate. Communicate. Communicate. The worst communication style is no communication. When people are left out of the loop, their imaginations often lead them to expect the worst. This is an energy waster.

- Dare to delegate, provide feedback, give ample credit to others, and be courageous. Fund raising is not for the faint of heart.

- Establish a personal support system within or even outside of your organization if possible. It might include your supervisor, a peer at another organization, or even a sympathetic volunteer.

- Encourage cautious risk taking. When I was a development director, I told my staff that if we never failed at anything, we weren't taking enough risks. Sometimes when people feel safe trying new things, their talents become more obvious, and they try harder.

A campaign manager may need support staff. There's no fast rule here. How many people you will need depends on the size of your campaign, the numbers of prospects, and so on. You may need one or more administrative assistants who work full or part time and perhaps even a full-time office manager in addition. It is often more cost effective to have support staff helping with the millions of tiny details, freeing you up for such tasks as working with your volunteers or planning solicitation strategies.

If your organization has never conducted a major gifts campaign before, Worksheet 2.4 will help you plan for adequate staffing by reviewing the size and results of your current development program. It's best to do your calculations in terms of FTE (full-time equivalent) positions. For example, your development staff might include three full-time professionals (3.0 FTE) and two half-time support staff (1.0 FTE). You must also take into account the anticipated length of the campaign. If you believe it will be six months and you need more staff, you will want to make sure they know the hiring is for a short-term position.

Assessing Your Organization's Database

An old fund raising sage once told me, "There are two things your organization never wants to lose—its reputation and its database." Now that you have identified the numbers of staff and volunteers needed in your campaign, the next important step is to assess the status of your current database. The importance of your database to successful fund raising cannot be emphasized too much. It should contain most if not all of the demographic information you have on your prospects and donors—including the correct spellings of their names, preferred salutations, listed and unlisted telephone numbers, and of course their giving histories. If you involve database staff in this review, make sure they understand you are not critiquing their work, just reviewing the information they have been given to work with. Make sure they understand they are valued members of your campaign team.

You also need to evaluate the adequacy of the software that manages your database. Can it be relied on to create reports that will likely need to contain key donor information to help volunteers with their solicitation

WORKSHEET 2.4

Reviewing Staff Needs

Enter the staff figures for a recent 12-month period and then use that information to estimate your needs for the major gifts campaign.

Time period: _____

	For a Recent 12-Month Period	For the Proposed Major Gifts Campaign
Number of fund raising managers (FTEs)	_____	_____
Number of support staff (FTEs)	_____	_____
Number of fund raising volunteers	_____	_____
Amount of money raised	_____	_____
Number of gifts	_____	_____

A REAL-LIFE STORY OF DATABASE REWARDS

I was working with a wonderful religious organization with a medieval gift processing system—a team of committed volunteers, an accounting ledger and a few two-ton typewriters. The members of this organization's vestry (board) were very conservative about money management. If they could recruit a volunteer, they were averse to hiring staff. Buying software seemed a waste of funds. But the situation changed when mistakes started happening and someone's mother got an acknowledgment letter that began "Dear Fred." I convinced the vestry by presenting a budget for a modest software program and an inexpensive plan to prepare all the data for conversion. Of course there would be a role for the volunteers. The conversion couldn't be done without them. Their job was to sort through all the index cards and paper trails of gifts going back forty years and to prepare individual records for each donor, on the typewriters of course. Because this organization operated in a small town, the volunteers knew most of the donors anyway. The process took over a year, eventually involved pro bono computer consultants, and was hugely successful. The original volunteer team said it was one of their most enjoyable projects ever. And the organization has now found a way to involve eager teenagers in its work—as information technology troubleshooters.

assignments—information such as nicknames; names of spouses, partners, and children; and interests? How well will it facilitate gift recording and acknowledging? Worksheet 2.5 begins your database review.

Not every nonprofit organization has stayed up to date with the technological revolution. Some have not yet joined that technological revolution. Some organizations still have donor information on index cards in file drawers. If you have been having a hard time getting your board to approve purchasing a software program for donor management, now you may have the right *opportunity* to convince them.

WORKSHEET 2.5

Reviewing Your Database

Complete this worksheet to get an overview of your current system, pinpointing potential trouble spots to deal with *now*, before the campaign starts.

Type of Information	Does It Exist Now?	Who Has It?	Where Is It?	How Long Does It Take to Get?	How Confident Am I About Its Accuracy?
Names, current addresses, and phone numbers of donors	_____	_____	_____	_____	_____
Names, current addresses, and phone numbers of potential donors	_____	_____	_____	_____	_____
Giving histories	_____	_____	_____	_____	_____
Accurate reports for specific types of gifts (for example, over $1,000) and for specific periods of time (for example, April 2001)	_____	_____	_____	_____	_____

Try these arguments. The right software can mean that volunteer solicitors, including board members, will have more accurate and up-to-date information about prospects and their giving histories. This can make it easier to recruit and retain good volunteers. The right software can mean increased accuracy and greater speed in gift acknowledgment, resulting in more satisfied donors and fewer embarrassing mistakes for the volunteers to hear about. And the right software can save time, allowing staff to spend more time raising money instead of managing an antiquated system.

Planning Your Campaign Materials

Many separate fund raising efforts—a spring appeal, capital campaign, planned giving program, or major gifts campaign—may require separate campaign material. This material is likely to include at least several versions of solicitation and acknowledgment letters, brochures, and a number of proposals written for different individual or institutional prospects that outline specific ways they can support your effort. Most major gifts campaigns need one or more documents that give prospects the answers to the key questions about the campaign case that appeared in the first worksheet in this chapter.

Campaign material has many purposes. It can present information to potential donors in visually appealing and compelling ways. Prospective donors and volunteers are more likely to read well-designed material. It can be a good tool to tell your organization's story. It can build the confidence of volunteers, reassuring them that they don't have to remember every last detail of the organization's information.

Deciding which general types of material to use can often be daunting. Thinking about what you want to accomplish can help. For example, printed materials may be preferable for the aspects of your organization's story that are best explained by charts and graphs. Videos may be best to showcase people who are wonderful advocates for your organization when they tell their stories in person. Videos and brochures are ideal for presenting compelling photographs. This might be especially desirable, for example, when the location of the need addressed by the campaign is far away or inaccessible to most people. Organizations whose campaign cases are already on a computer can use computer software to insert photographs and other graphics into these documents. A Web site may be the best way to communicate with others when you want to update information monthly, weekly, or even daily.

Whatever types of material you choose, follow these guidelines to communicate effectively with donors about what they want to know:

- Avoid jargon. People may hesitate to support a campaign if they can't understand what you've written.

CHOOSING MATERIALS: PRACTICAL CONSIDERATIONS

Material	Cost	Time to Produce	Pros	Cons
Printed brochure	From a few cents to well over $1.00 per brochure, depending on number, designer fees, stock, graphics, and so forth; plus staff time to write and coordinate.	Can take several weeks or even months.	Easy-to-distribute, visual way to convey program; colorful and graphic; photos make the program appear very human.	Once printed, cannot be changed easily unless computerized, and in that case, quality may be compromised; one size fits all—it can't be personalized for each prospect.
Campaign case (entered into a computer)	Staff time to gather data, think through the campaign, and convey the benefits to the donors.	Several weeks or longer.	It is *the* most important document your campaign will have; can be personalized for each prospect with an individualized ask; simple to edit and update	If you don't have time to create a campaign case, you don't have time to conduct a campaign.
Letters	Staff time.	Minimal.	Can be used to request meetings, follow up on questions, and so forth.	As a stand-alone, not the most effective way to solicit major gifts.
Video	As much as $10,000 or more per final minute; significant staff time even if outside videographer is used.	Usually months.	Can be taken to the prospect's home or office; visual and "real" way to see the organization.	Costly to change once completed.
Web site	Varies considerably; usually created as a separate page of the organization's main Web site.	Depends on sophistication of multimedia: photos, graphics, streaming video, and so on.	Easy to access for on-line prospects; modern and up to date; easier to update than brochures or video.	Difficult to know if the prospect has viewed it; distribution limited to prospects on-line; e-mail addresses may change.

- Emphasize community benefits. Remember, nobody cares about your organization's need for new computers. But people may care that the new computers will enable the organization to keep more accurate records of clients' health conditions and better manage their care. Always connect the goals of the campaign back to your mission.

- Describe how donors' gifts will be used. Give enough detail so people can understand right away what the money they give will be used for and how this will help the organization meet its mission and thus serve the community better.

- Tell prospects why the campaign is important now. Urgency can be a strong selling point.

- Use simple charts and graphics when you can to replace complex or detailed explanations. They can be more persuasive than words alone.

- Use pictures of people. They're why your organization is conducting this campaign in the first place. Tell their stories.

- Beware of colored text. It's often hard to read printing in certain colors—red and yellow, for example. Make it easy on your readers.

- Make sure all print is large enough to be read easily. This is especially important for older donors or those with limited vision.

Use Worksheet 2.6 to create a list of all the types of material your organization uses now and consider the types you are likely to need for the major gifts campaign.

Checklist for Success

Here's a handy checklist (Worksheet 2.7) of all your get-ready things to do. Check them off as you complete them. If there are any you can't get done, you are not ready to move ahead. Go back and give yourself more time, to ensure a successful campaign in the future.

This chapter has shown you how case development ties into the Fund Raising Cycle and how it extends into a major gifts campaign. It has introduced concepts about staffing and people management that are especially important to be conscious of when you are managing your first campaign. It has described how critical your database and the team that manages it are to your success. And it has tried to impress upon you the vital importance of effective and ongoing communication throughout your organization. Finally, it has given you ways to think about the kinds of material you want to use to solicit prospective donors. Now you're ready to set some goals.

WORKSHEET 2.6

Selecting Campaign Materials

Evaluate each of the following materials for their impact on your campaign. Decide which will work best for you and who will be responsible for creating them.

	Video	Web Site	Printed Brochure	Campaign Case	Other (specify)	Other (specify)
Have now	_____	_____	_____	_____	_____	_____
Good for new campaign	_____	_____	_____	_____	_____	_____
Who should do it	_____	_____	_____	_____	_____	_____
Cost	_____	_____	_____	_____	_____	_____
Start date	_____	_____	_____	_____	_____	_____
Completion date	_____	_____	_____	_____	_____	_____

WORKSHEET 2.7

Checklist for Success

	Yes, I Have It	No, I Don't Have It Yet	I Have Plans to Get It	I Have a Timeline for Getting It	I Have Identified the People I Need to Work With to Get It
Internal case	_____	_____	_____	_____	_____
Campaign case and other campaign material	_____	_____	_____	_____	_____
Fund raising software	_____	_____	_____	_____	_____
People to use the software	_____	_____	_____	_____	_____
Support staff	_____	_____	_____	_____	_____

CHAPTER 3

Setting Goals

YOUR MAJOR GIFTS CAMPAIGN has two goals, one is a programs and services goal that helps you meet your mission. The other is financial. It is the financial goal that enables your programs and services goal. This chapter deals with your financial goal. With a carefully determined and realistic financial goal, you can increase the confidence of your volunteers and donors that your campaign is headed for success and then achieve that success. Conversely, unrealistic goals can create concerns in the minds of volunteers and donors, who generally do not want to get involved in an effort they think may fail.

Using the worksheets in this chapter will get you started on drafting a prospect list, which you will then complete in Chapter Four, "Identifying, Qualifying, and Rating Potential Donors."

Creating a Gift Chart

An important early step in goal setting is the construction of a gift chart, or table of gift levels. (Use Worksheet 3.1a.) An essential use of the gift chart is to demonstrate that you have an adequate number of qualified prospects at each gift level before you start your campaign. Lack of adequate prospects is one of the main reasons campaigns fail to meet their goals.

The top gift on the ideal chart is usually equal to 10 to 20 percent of the organization's campaign goal. At the next level down, it will show prospective donors for two or more gifts of a somewhat lesser amount, and so on. Gifts decrease in amount going from the top to the bottom. Conversely, the number of prospects usually increases from top to bottom.

The best way to create your gift chart is to begin with the total amount of money you *would like* to raise. Then divide this goal into different-sized gifts in various levels, making sure the total on the chart equals your campaign's initial goal. Usually the development officer is given this initial goal by the executive director, and it represents the budget for a special purpose. Remember, however, that this may not end up being the actual campaign goal. At this stage in your campaign planning, it is just a starting point.

GIFT CHART FOR A TYPICAL $500,000 MAJOR GIFTS CAMPAIGN

Number of Gifts	Gift Level	Number of Prospects	Cumulative Number of Prospects	Total at This Level	Cumulative Total
1	$100,000+	4	4	$100,000	$100,000
2	50,000–99,000	8	12	100,000+	200,000+
5	25,000–49,000	20	32	125,000+	325,000+
8	10,000–24,000	32	64	80,000+	405,000+
10	$1,000–9,000	40	104	10,000+	415,000+
Many	< 1,000	Many	200+	85,000	500,000

WORKSHEET 3.1a

Creating Your Own Gift Chart

Complete this blank version of the gift chart illustrated earlier. In the second column, enter the gift levels appropriate for your campaign. Remember that the number of prospects should increase as the gift levels decrease in dollar amounts.

Number of Gifts	Gift Level	Number of Prospects	Cumulative Number of Prospects	Total at This Level	Cumulative Total
_____	_____	_____	_____	_____	_____
_____	_____	_____	_____	_____	_____
_____	_____	_____	_____	_____	_____
_____	_____	_____	_____	_____	_____
_____	_____	_____	_____	_____	_____
_____	_____	_____	_____	_____	_____
_____	_____	_____	_____	_____	_____

Next develop a preliminary prospect list for your major gifts campaign. (Use Worksheet 3.1b.) Go over your organization's database of donors and potential donors. Seek information from the board's development committee and other key volunteers. Ask them to review your list and comment on names and likely gifts. Ideally, as your campaign progresses, you will be expanding this list as you involve campaign leaders and other volunteers who can be a source of additional names. This list will give you an early assessment of your campaign's financial potential. It will also help you determine a feasible goal for your campaign.

WORKSHEET 3.1b

Constructing a Preliminary Prospect List

Make a list of your potential major gifts donors, writing down their names and likely gift amounts in the appropriate columns. Total the gift amounts. Because not all prospects will give, the total should be significantly more than your goal.

Prospect Name	Likely Gift Amount
_____	_____
_____	_____
_____	_____
_____	_____
_____	_____
_____	_____
_____	_____
_____	_____
_____	_____
_____	_____
_____	_____
_____	_____
_____	_____
_____	_____
_____	_____
_____	TOTAL $ _____

Now create a campaign pyramid, referring to Figure 3.1 as a model, to determine how many prospects you have at each gift level. (Use Worksheet 3.1c.) This activity will also help you visualize your campaign as a series of tiered, consecutive tasks and plan accordingly.

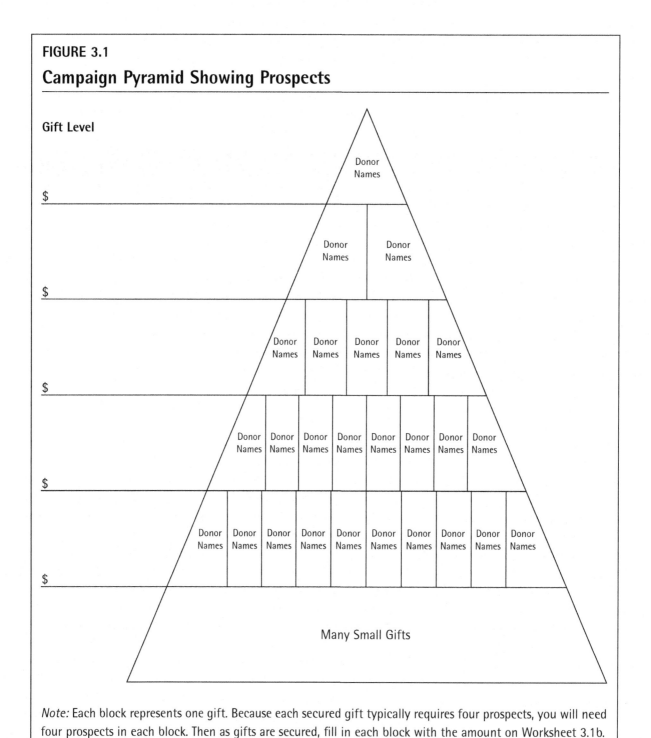

FIGURE 3.1

Campaign Pyramid Showing Prospects

Gift Level

Note: Each block represents one gift. Because each secured gift typically requires four prospects, you will need four prospects in each block. Then as gifts are secured, fill in each block with the amount on Worksheet 3.1b.

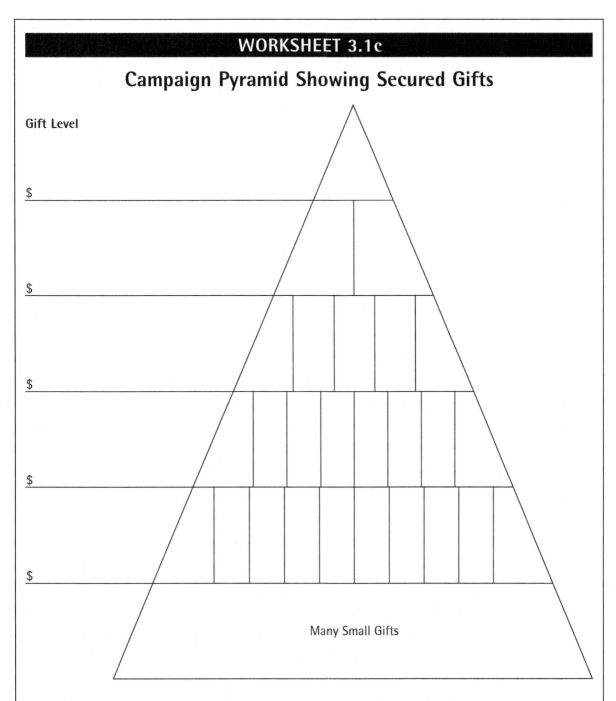

WORKSHEET 3.1c

Campaign Pyramid Showing Secured Gifts

Gift Level

$ _____

$ _____

$ _____

$ _____

$ _____

Many Small Gifts

Note: As each gift is secured, shade in one block on the appropriate level, noting the actual gift amount and donor name. You will likely have different amounts in any one level. Alter the number of levels as necessary to make the pyramid fit your campaign.

To feel confident about reaching your goal, you should have four prospects for each major gift. In other words, if you expect two gifts at a certain level, you should have eight prospects for those two gifts. Only some of the prospects you identify will actually give at that level. Some will give a lesser amount, and some will decide to give nothing or will not be willing to meet with your organization's representative.

Responding When the Total Is Less Than You Need

Notice the holes in your gift chart where there are no or not enough prospects. If you are lucky enough to have more than enough prospects at the higher levels, remember that not all of them will give at that level and some will probably fall down into the lower levels. If you have significant holes in the upper level of the chart, especially in the top three levels, you would be wise to rethink your planning and perhaps your goal. Have you done a thorough review of your donor database? Mailing lists? Lists of donors to similar organizations in your community? Have you included every current member of your board, former board members, and other volunteers? Have you involved your staff, board, other volunteers, and key donors in prospecting? If not, work further on your prospect list. If so, lower your campaign goal to reflect the prospects you have now. Remember, the organization's need does not determine the goal. Reality determines the goal.

Although it is wise to stretch a little, your ultimate campaign goal should reflect the reality of the results of your fund raising program at the present and how far you can likely expand those results for this campaign. If you determine, based on current information, that the goal given you is not feasible, you must immediately make your assessment known. The people responsible for program budgeting should create a new goal, one based on your informed recommendations. Perhaps the project can be reduced in scope or perhaps certain elements can be postponed. If anyone important to your success, like your supervisor, executive director, or board president, tells you to try to "raise the money anyway," take caution. This is a giant red flag that must not be ignored. This is an important time for you to be firm in your convictions and to state your opinions loud and clear. Trying to meet an unrealistic goal can damage the credibility of your organization and hurt its relationships with its present donors and volunteers.

Using the Gift Chart to Plan the Campaign

As you can see, the first use of the gift chart is as a reality check. Does your organization's goal reflect its reality?

A second but critical use of the gift chart is to help you visualize your campaign as a series of sequential campaigns, each subsequent effort focusing on smaller-sized gifts. You begin with the donors of the top gifts because they set the sights for other donors. If you can solicit individuals by telling them that a lead gift of $100,000 has been received for your $500,000 campaign, your prospects will quickly see how important the campaign is and how likely it is to succeed. Likewise, if you can tell a $5,000 potential contributor that ten gifts of $10,000 have already been raised, that may help her see that the campaign is important enough for her to give $5,000.

Once your campaign begins, you can begin to fill in the blocks shown in Worksheet 3.1c as the gifts are pledged or given. At this point you need only one secured gift for every four prospects. At each volunteer meeting pass out an updated gift chart. This way, your volunteers can take pride in seeing more and more of the blocks filled in, each representing one secured gift. This is also a good way for the staff to monitor the success of the campaign.

In this chapter, you have learned how to set a realistic campaign goal that will help your volunteers and potential donors develop confidence in your effort. I have also illustrated the elements of the gift chart, which will help you plan and monitor your campaign. You are now ready to delve more deeply into creating an expanded list of qualified and rated potential contributors.

CHAPTER 4

Identifying, Qualifying, and Rating Potential Donors

IN THIS CHAPTER you will learn techniques and strategies for identification of the potential donors you will need if your organization is to meet the goals you set in the previous chapter. You will learn how to involve your current donors in your major gifts campaign, even if they do not want to serve on a campaign committee.

Understanding What Makes a Major Gifts Prospect

Three things generally qualify an individual as a major gifts prospect. They are listed here in order of importance. First, the person has some *connection* or *linkage* to the organization or to someone involved in the organization. Even though a person may be well known in your community as one of its wealthiest people, she may not be a realistic prospect unless you can engage her in your project. You or someone sympathetic to your organization should have reason to believe that the potential donor is likely to respond to invitations, speak with you by phone, or agree to a meeting. Remember, major gifts are ideally solicited in individual, face-to-face meetings, so you need more than someone's mailing address before you can confidently seek their support.

Second, the person must have *the ability* to contribute a major gift, either immediately or paid over a specific time set by the campaign leaders.

Third, the person must have a *belief* or *interest* in your cause. Of course the best evidence that someone believes in your cause is that he is already a donor or volunteer for your organization or for an organization like it.

People often refer to these three characteristics as LAI (linkage, ability, and interest). When you are reasonably certain that someone meets the LAI requirements, you have *qualified* that person as a major gift prospect.

Why You Can't Solicit Everyone for a Major Gift

Because nonprofit organizations must make careful use of their resources, it is necessary to determine which individuals are the best prospects for a major gifts campaign. Otherwise, limited resources such as staff and volunteer time may be wasted on prospects who are *un*likely to make major gifts. Moreover, perhaps even more important, volunteers and staff working on the major gifts effort may become demoralized by the low return on their efforts. When this happens, it can become harder to recruit and motivate volunteers. Organizations may then adopt a can't-do attitude about raising major gifts even though the problem is not a lack of fund raising ability or of good prospects but a failure to identify those good prospects carefully enough.

In the last chapter you identified enough possible donors to set your financial goal. Now that work needs to be taken further to identify more prospects and then learn more about all your potential donors to select those most likely to assist you. The process of coming up with potential donors is called, not surprisingly, *prospecting.* Begin by considering all the sources you might use for prospect names (in Worksheet 4.1).

You might also find it useful to imagine a dart board with several concentric circles. These circles represent all the people within your organization's reach or likely sphere of influence.

The smallest circle is the one closest to the center. It contains the smallest number of people but what makes it so important is that these are the people who are your organization's immediate family. That is, they are the one's *already involved* with its work. They are the board members, other volunteers, staff, donors, members, and participants.

The second concentric circle, which is a little larger, includes people who have not given before but who are connected to people who are involved with your organization and who are likely to be interested in its cause. These new people might be friends, neighbors, or business associates of those who are already part of your family.

The third and largest circle includes people who are known to be interested in your organization's cause but who are not currently known by anyone in the family. Perhaps they are well known in the community as supportive of causes like yours or their names show up on the published donor lists of like-minded organizations.

It is relatively easy to prepare a list of prospects from your inner circle. You are likely to know these people and something about them already.

To canvass the second circle thoroughly, you must involve members of the inner circle. You might, for example, hand out lined sheets of paper at

WORKSHEET 4.1

Locating Sources of Names

Read the following sources of names of possible donors for your campaign and then add your own source suggestions. Give the completed list as a research aid to your volunteers who are assisting you with identifying prospective donors.

Personal	Business	Community	Family
Address book	Chamber of Commerce	Service groups	Family members
Holiday card list	Professional associations	Churches, temples, mosques	Parents of children's friends
Alumni associations	Colleagues	Neighborhood associations	PTAs
Private clubs	Employees	Donor lists for local campaigns	Camp rosters
Hobby clubs	Vendors	Teachers	
_____	_____	_____	_____
_____	_____	_____	_____
_____	_____	_____	_____
_____	_____	_____	_____

a board meeting and ask members to take fifteen minutes to write down the names of prospective donors they are acquainted with or know of. Be sure to collect all these lists at the meeting so you can guard the confidentiality of the information the board members are giving (and also to ensure you get the lists back). It may be necessary to assure the board members that providing names does not mean they will be required to solicit these prospects. Indeed, ideally each list will be far too big for that. The same process can be carried out with members of various committees, staff, and donors (a process discussed in more detail later in this chapter).

Once you have gathered a list of names from the second circle with the help of members of the inner circle, you need to consider ways to get names from the third circle. Remember, these are people who support similar organizations but who are not yet known to you. One of the best ways to identify them is to review donor lists. It is important to remember here that *no one organization owns any donor.* Donors typically enjoy supporting many organizations and causes. And organizations have every right to try to cultivate relationships with them and solicit them. Simply make a list of these like-minded groups, get their telephone numbers, and call each one up to request a copy of its most recent annual report, which most likely will list the names of individual donors by gift size. If you or others you have asked to help are uncomfortable about this, it may help to remember that annual reports are produced solely to distribute to the public. Groups want people to know about their programs and annual accomplishments. And certainly other groups are reading any donor lists published by your organization.

Finally, all the names you have collected in these various processes should be arranged in a master list that a staff member is responsible for maintaining.

Determining How Much You Can Ask Prospects to Give

Now that you have a list of qualified major gift prospects (that is, people who have connections or linkages to your organization, the ability to make a significant gift, and a belief or interest in its cause), you must *rate* these individuals according to their likely gift size. This is a very important part of your planning; you must identify the people on whom you are going to concentrate your efforts and your scarce resources.

Rating can be done in different ways and can involve different groups of people. One way is simply to ask staff to look at the list of the prospects and make their best guess as to the amount each will likely give. However, you are likely to gain more accurate information if you involve your board members, other volunteers, and donors.

For instance, you might create a special committee of people who agree to act as prospect raters and to meet with you individually or as a group throughout your campaign, depending on the need. Or you might carry out prospect rating as an item on your board meeting's agenda. Hand out a list of prospects to the board members so they can discuss each name and determine a likely gift amount. This information can then be added to the master list.

In addition, asking a few well-connected donors or volunteers to meet with you privately may be helpful, especially when knowledgeable people are hesitant about revealing personal information about others in a larger meeting. One way to do this is to prepare an alphabetical list of the prospects you want to discuss. The list may also include information like city of residence if that seems helpful. Call or write the donors or volunteers you want to learn from to ask if you might stop by their homes or offices to have a confidential meeting with them in order to help your campaign succeed. Be sure to tell them you would like them to review a short list at that time to determine your best prospects. Assure them that you will maintain not only the confidentiality of the information but also its sources.

Take enough copies of the list so that everyone present has a copy to look at and that you have one to write on. Go down the list, name by name, writing down participants' comments about the likelihood of getting a gift from each person and at what dollar level and any other pertinent information. Be sure when you leave to take all copies with you. No one outside of your close inner circle (board members, key campaign volunteers, and a few staff) should ever have a copy of your prospect list. Although these kinds of rating meetings may seem time-consuming, the value of the information you receive can be considerable.

After you complete this process with several different people, you will create an amalgamated or combined list with all of the information. (Again, this is a highly confidential list. Do not let it sit around your office.) It is at this point that a final decision may be made as to the amount each person will be asked. Remember that after you have cultivated relationships with potential donors and informed them about your campaign's goals, the amount you request may change. However, you still want to give your solicitors an idea of an initial amount to ask for. Remember that volunteers hate to guess how much to ask someone to give. They are afraid the prospect

---

SAMPLE LETTER REQUESTING PROSPECT REVIEW MEETING

Dear Ms. Garcia:

Thank you again for your support of XYZ Organization. You are one of our most loyal volunteers. We are especially pleased to let you know that we believe we have an opportunity to expand our work and serve more people. To do this, we must conduct a major gifts campaign to pay for the needed improvements.

To ensure the campaign's success, we are speaking with a few people who may be able to share some information about some of our potential contributors. We would like to ask you for a private meeting in your home during which we will ask you to comment on a list of people. All information will be kept absolutely confidential as will your participation. Be assured that we will tell no one, especially those whom we may solicit, the source of our information.

I will call you next week to see if you might be able to spend approximately one hour with us sometime during the next month.

Thank you again for your efforts to help us serve our community.

Sincerely,

Jane Smith
Development Director

A REAL-LIFE STORY OF INVOLVEMENT INCREASING GIVING

One small arts organization sent a letter to a loyal $1,000 donor whom they had tried unsuccessfully to recruit to their board. After the woman agreed to a meeting, the development director and a consultant went to the donor's house with the list of potential donors, a bottle of wine, and a small plate of crackers and cheese purchased from the deli counter of a supermarket. In the ninety-minute meeting, the woman not only spontaneously expressed an interest in personally supporting the campaign but also identified an individual who had just acquired significant wealth through a business transaction. That individual eventually committed a $100,000 gift to the campaign over a three-year period.

---

will be offended by an amount that is either way too high or way too low. Confident volunteers are almost always more willing to solicit than those who are unsure.

By this time the master list that staff are maintaining will probably have at least six columns. For each prospect it might tell you the name, city, amount to ask for, the likelihood that the person will make a gift, the person's likely reasons for giving (interests, beliefs), and the sources of your information.

Hiring a Research Firm or Consultant

Sometimes it is advisable to ask professional researchers to help you identify the prospects most likely to make big gifts. They may assist you in one or both of two ways. They can do an electronic screening of your donor database to help you determine which ones are most worth soliciting for major gifts. Or they can conduct in-depth research of a smaller list of names, going beyond the organization's resources.

The first service is usually offered by research firms rather than individual consultants because it requires a certain level of technological capacity. The firm is likely to charge $1 or more per record, with a minimum charge of $10,000 or more. If your organization meets one or both of the following criteria, you may want to consider this service. First, your goal is significant enough to warrant this expense. Second, you believe you do not have the internal capacity to determine which prospects are the most likely to give. Many organizations that have geographically dispersed donors—for example, alumni associations or nonprofits that operate throughout the nation—may fall into this category.

Usually the research firm will indicate which of the people on your list are most qualified to give at a certain level or above. Some firms, however, may rate each individual according to a numbered scale. For example, each name might be assigned a score between 1 and 25, with 25 indicating the greatest likelihood of making a major gift and 1 the least likelihood.

TAKING THE GUESSWORK OUT OF RATING

In addition to the information you get from individuals such as staff, other donors, and board members, you can take these steps to make sure your volunteers have good information.

- Review your organization's database for information. Don't just look at the biggest gift the donor has ever made and assume that is the amount you should request. It may have been given in response to a circumstance that is unlikely to be repeated, like a financial windfall or inheritance. It may even be way too small.

- Consider how previous gifts were solicited. If the donor gave $5,000 to you in response to a direct-mail letter, a $5,000 request for your major gifts campaign may be too small. If that $5,000 gift was solicited by a close friend of the donor who is no longer involved with your organization, a similar request may be too large.

- Look at what your prospects have given to other organizations. Of course a $1 million gift to another organization does not ensure the same gift for yours. You may be even more important to the donor and might ask for more!

- Be knowledgeable about personal circumstances that affect ability to give. Have twin sons just gone off to an expensive university? Has a primary wage earner in the family been unable to work for a significant period of time?

- Has the prospect been closely involved with your organization? How recent was this involvement? Has the prospect had any conversations with representatives of your organization that suggest the prospect's level of enthusiasm and areas of interest?

- Have you cultivated relationships with your prospects? Sometimes prospects who have ongoing relationships with your organization will help you determine how much to ask. At some point they might tell you, "We want to do something really big this time," or "We want to be the lead donor."

RATING PITFALLS TO AVOID

- Dividing up the goal by the number of prospects, and asking everyone for the same amount.

- Assuming that big houses and upscale lifestyles determine major gift capacity.

- Assuming that small houses and modest lifestyles preclude major gift capacity.

- Assuming that the people who are currently your largest donors will remain so.

- Assuming that people who are currently your smallest donors will remain so.

In-depth analysis of a small list of prospects is offered by both research firms and individual researchers. It is typical to pay between $100 and $150 per name for this service. The information you receive on an individual donor can be significant and may include names of spouses or partners and children, educational background, employment background, board and business affiliations, types of investments, net worth projections, real estate owned, and so on.

A common procedure among nonprofits is to hire a large firm to do an electronic screening of a large list of records. Then the individual researcher who does more intensive research can work with the much smaller list of donors who seem the most promising based on the larger review.

Some organizations have concerns about acquiring so much seemingly personal information about individuals. However, it is neither unethical nor illegal. It is all publicly available information and is drawn from such sources as the Internet, newspapers, magazines, and public records. Still, every nonprofit organization has to decide for itself whether it wants to use professional research services.

Keeping Track of Your Findings

Make sure you keep careful records on all your prospects, pulling together information from various sources. Develop a list of information categories, such as the one shown here, to assist with organizing the material and checking that you have addressed all the key categories. You will want to create individual file folders for some key prospects. These files may include newspaper articles and copies of communications with them and about them. This information will be extremely helpful when you begin to develop strategies for cultivation and solicitation, topics covered in Chapters Seven and Eight. Even if you do not solicit all your prospects for this campaign, the information should be kept for future use.

PROSPECT INFORMATION SHEET—CONFIDENTIAL

Use these headings for your prospect information sheet:

Prospect name(s)	Children/family
Address (home and office)	Giving history to our organization
Phone	Giving history to other organizations
Fax	Other involvement with our organization
E-mail	(volunteering, subscribing)
Occupation	Community activities
Title	Names of people connected to us who are
Employer	connected to this prospect
Employer address	Why we think the prospect is interested in our cause
Source of income (earned and unearned)	Approximate size of request
Prospect's interests	Sources of information for this sheet
Spouse/partner	Date sheet was filled out
Spouse/partner's interests	Name of person filling out this sheet

---

In this chapter you learned how to find potential donors, how to determine whether they might be interested in your campaign, and how to determine how much they might be asked to donate. It is important to complete the worksheets presented in this chapter and in Chapter Three and a master list of prospects before moving on to the chapters on cultivation and solicitation.

PROS AND CONS OF DIFFERENT WAYS TO RATE PROSPECTS

Rating Sources	Cost	Time	Pros	Cons
Professional firm screening computer database	$1 to $2 per name.	Two weeks or more.	Can quickly assess large database; can provide names for next process.	Can be costly; some may be uncomfortable with process.
Professional individual researcher	$100 to $150 per name.	Can take several weeks to do list of less than 100 names.	Can provide significant detailed information.	Same as above.
Board of directors	Time of staff to manage.	Two or more meetings, depending on absences of key people at first meeting.	Can increase buy-in of board; helps determine who has best connections to prospects.	Some may feel uncomfortable with process.
Campaign committee	Staff time; minimal hospitality costs.	Most effective if done early in campaign; also can be ongoing throughout campaign.	Can be effective way to increase your organization's sphere of influence; can be excellent way to test volunteers' level of interest; helps determine which committee members might solicit which prospects.	Volunteers may get tired after more than one meeting; some volunteers may help only if assured they will not have to solicit any of the names.
Individual donors or volunteers in private meetings	Staff time; minimal hospitality costs.	Best if done early in campaign.	Many people are more forthcoming in private meetings.	Busy schedules may mean delays in getting information if you rely on a small number of people.
Staff	Staff time.	Ongoing.	Can be efficient use of staff time.	Is generally less effective; fails to involve volunteers and test their commitment.

Understanding Why Budgeting Is Important

The 1-2-3-4 of the Budgeting Process

How Much Your Campaign Should Cost

Figuring Out What Things Will Cost

Drafting Your Budget

Monitoring and Correcting Your Budget

Paying for Expenses

CHAPTER 5

Budgeting for Your Campaign

BUDGETING IS A PLANNING AND MANAGEMENT TOOL. Limited resources force you to make hard choices between different options. Budgeting helps you decide how to use your limited resources in the most effective way. Having a realistic and well thought out budget *before* you actively begin your campaign will prevent many headaches later on. This chapter shows you how to estimate costs, work with other people in your organization who are important to the process, and monitor your budget.

Understanding Why Budgeting Is Important

You want potential donors to invest in your campaign. Like all investors, before they invest they want to know how your campaign manages its funds. And this means how it manages expenses as well as income. If you underestimate campaign expenses and incur additional costs, this may reduce the amount of money available for the purpose of your campaign. If as a result of such underestimation the financial goal needs to be raised, you may lose the confidence and commitment of your donors and volunteers. And you may lose your supervisor's confidence in your overall ability. Therefore consider budgeting just as critical to your campaign's success as soliciting. Your donors will be happy when you do.

The 1-2-3-4 of the Budgeting Process

Budgeting involves four basic steps. They are, in order:

1. Prepare a budget for the entire campaign.

2. Compare actual costs with estimates throughout the campaign. You might do this monthly or as often as you think necessary.

3. Analyze the variances (differences) between the estimates and the actual figures. Ask yourself such questions as, Why did this expense come in higher or lower than expected? How might this difference affect the rest of the budget?

4. Take corrective action. This may mean trimming other costs (before they are incurred!), relying on pro bono assistance or in-kind contributions, or even increasing the budget.

A REAL-LIFE STORY OF BEING WILLING TO ASK FOR HELP

Once there was a campaign director who was confident about her abilities in most areas, but budgeting was not one of them. She was embarrassed to admit her weakness to her supervisor. So she created what she called an "intellectual treasure hunt." Who in her organization might be able to help her? She immediately thought of three people—the chief financial officer, the project manager for a recently completed building renovation, and the chair of the board's finance committee. For various reasons she didn't want to ask any of them. Then it dawned on her— a member of her own development committee was a retired business owner who, she believed, was more interested in finance than in fund raising. In fact he often came to committee meetings late, left early, and had expressed his perception that the organization lacked good business sense. She called him up and asked if he would help her develop her budget and teach her how to monitor it. He agreed. His help turned out to be critical, as cost overruns in other departments meant her budget was cut just as the campaign began. As a result of their partnership, her campaign came in below the reduced budget, and the volunteer became chair of the finance committee.

How Much Your Campaign Should Cost

Major gifts campaigns are among the most cost-effective fund raising efforts. It is usually much less costly per dollar raised to bring in $100,000 from a few major gifts than to raise the same sum from a special event or from a direct-mail campaign, either of which may have expenses larger than income.

In my experience, major gifts campaigns generally cost from 5 to 15 percent of the dollars raised. Two key indicators of where your total expense will fall are the overall goal of the campaign and your organization's history with major gifts.

Like most undertakings, major gifts campaigns can exhibit economies of scale. For example, although you may edit it as the campaign progresses, you usually write your campaign case only once. So the cost of preparing this document may be the same whether your goal is $100,000 or $1 million. In addition, your organization's previous experience with major gifts usually influences the campaign cost. If you have a large list of current or former major donors, if you have volunteers already involved who have cultivated and solicited some of the key prospects during earlier efforts, if you have kept your already identified prospects well informed and involved, you are ahead of the game and may need to spend less time doing research, identifying and recruiting volunteers, and so on. So it might cost your organization 15 percent ($15,000) to raise $100,000, but only 5 percent ($250,000) to raise $5 million.

Although there are exceptions, small to medium-sized organizations with campaign goals under $1 million should plan on spending a minimum of 10 percent of the dollars raised for their expenses.

Many organizations feel uncomfortable about including staff salaries and benefits in their campaign budgets. Although this is understandable, it is always best to include *all* the costs. Since the biggest costs are typically for personnel, staff, and consultants, including these expenses educates volunteers and donors about the *real* cost of fund raising.

Figuring Out What Things Will Cost

You do not have to be a financial whiz to prepare and monitor a budget. But you *do* have to be conscientious, realistic, and thorough. And it helps if you have some history to go on. Here are some easy preliminary steps.

1. Get copies of past fund raising budgets if available. You may have to ask people in the development department and the finance office for this information, or even former staff.

2. Ask the people who created these budgets how they estimated the expenses. Review the differences, if any, between the estimated and actual expenses. Ask how any significant variances happened and what could be done in the future to prevent them.

3. Talk to your peers at other organizations. (I find that fund raisers are, by nature, very collegial.)

4. Take a workshop. If your community does not have nonprofit management and training, check the offerings at your community college.

5. Read more books. I particularly recommend Chapter Five, titled "Developing Budgets," in *Securing Your Organization's Future* (Seltzer, 1987) and the weighty *Financial Management in Nonprofit Organizations* (Wacht, 1991).

Consider this example of a budget for a $1 million major gifts campaign that is expected to last one year.

TWELVE-MONTH BUDGET FOR A $1 MILLION CAMPAIGN

Income

	Individuals	$800,000	
	Foundations	100,000	
	Corporations	50,000	
	Other: service clubs	50,000	
		TOTAL	$1,000,000

Expenses

Personnel

	Executive director @ 10% including benefits	10,000	
	Development director @ 50% including benefits	35,000	
	Support staff: new, full-time campaign assistant including benefits	35,000	
	Consultant(s): fund raising	10,000	
		TOTAL PERSONNEL	$90,000

Communications

	Brochure (includes printing)	5,000	
	Video	15,000	
	Newsletters (includes printing)	Part of department's budget	
	Web site (includes Web master)	Part of organization's budget	
	Invitations	500	
	Signs, displays, picture boards	500	
		TOTAL COMMUNICATIONS	21,000

Research

	Consultant	3,000	
	Firm		
		TOTAL RESEARCH	$3,000

Special events

	Admission-free cultivation	1,000	
	Admission-free, large public kickoff	4,000	
	Large community fund raising	0	
		TOTAL EVENTS	$5,000

Miscellaneous printing

	Pledge cards	100	
	Invitations	500	
	Other	0	
		TOTAL PRINTING	$600

Donor stewardship and recognition

	Donor plaques	1,250	
	Tours	Covered by hospitality	
	Hospitality	700	
		TOTAL STEWARDSHIP AND RECOGNITION	$1,950

Volunteer management

	Packets	100	
	Training	1,000	
	Hospitality	1,500	
	Recognition	1,000	
		TOTAL VOLUNTEER MANAGEMENT	$3,600
		SUBTOTAL	$125,150
Contingency @ 10%		12,515	
		GRAND TOTAL	$137,665
			(13.76% of the campaign goal)

The sample budget looks nice and tidy. But how do you come up with the actual estimates? Think of each expense as a stew of smaller expenses. List each of those smaller ingredients. Don't be afraid of being too detailed. Having too many details is usually better than not having enough. The following sections provide some practical assistance by illustrating how to estimate personnel costs and the costs of a brochure.

Calculating the Biggest Part of Your Budget—Personnel

Nonprofits are labor-intensive organizations. And fund raising is one of the most labor-intensive activities there is. Here are some key questions to help you determine personnel costs.

Can you conduct this campaign with the people currently employed by your organization? Can their hours be increased to accommodate the extra workload? Have they finished another project so they will be free to do this one? If not, then you will probably have to hire additional help.

If you do need to hire additional staff or consultants, what role(s) will they have? Prospect researcher? Fund raising consultant? Support person? If you are hiring consultants, meet with several candidates and ask how much they would charge. Remember, the person offering the lowest quote is not necessarily the best one for the job.

How much time will the executive director need to spend on the campaign? The sample budget calculated the campaign would take 10 percent of the director's time. But if the director is deeply involved with the fund raising, it may take 50 percent of his or her time, and the organization may need additional support staff to free up that time. If the gift accounting staff is already overburdened, you may need to hire a data entry person for the campaign's duration.

How much time will the campaign manager need to spend on the campaign? If this person already has other full-time responsibilities, you *must* promptly address ways to free up this person's time too. Campaigns can't be managed in a spare moment or two. Consider hiring additional support staff or a consultant.

Here is a sample of how you might calculate key personnel expenses for the hours these staff spend on the twelve-month, $1 million major gifts campaign budget illustrated earlier.

CALCULATING PERSONNEL EXPENSES (SAMPLE)	
Executive director	
Number of anticipated hours	200
Cost per hour	$50
Total executive director expense	$10,000
Finance director	
Number of anticipated hours	None
Development director	
Number of anticipated hours	1,000
Cost per hour	$35
Total development director expense	$35,000
Campaign manager	
Will not be necessary to hire a separate campaign manager	
Support staff #1	
Number of anticipated hours	2,000
Cost per hour	$17.50
No other support staff necessary	
Total support staff expense	$35,000
Fund raising consultant	
Number of anticipated hours	100
Cost per hour	$100
Total consultant expense	$10,000
TOTAL PERSONNEL EXPENSE	$90,000

Now try calculating the likely personnel expenses for your own major gifts campaign. (Use Exhibit 5.1.)

Estimating the Costs for a Brochure

To estimate the costs for printed matter, such as a brochure, recall what I said earlier about listing each of the ingredients that make up an item's cost. A brochure has several individual expenses—design, type setting, photography, paper, and printing. If you hire a designer, he or she may be able to develop the entire budget for the brochure. But remember, you are still the person responsible for the overall campaign budget.

Here is an exercise to help you think about the decisions you will have to make about your brochure (see Exhibit 5.2 on p. 54). These decisions will in turn affect the cost estimate you will put in your overall campaign budget.

EXHIBIT 5.1

Calculating Personnel Expenses

For each position on this list, you will need to obtain the base salary and the cost of benefits in order to determine the position's cost per hour. (Remember, some executive directors have a benefits package different from that for other staff.) Enter your estimate of the hours the person will need to spend on the major gifts campaign, enter the cost per hour, and then multiply these two figures to obtain the amount that should be charged to the campaign as a fund raising expense.

Executive director
   Number of anticipated hours   _____
   Cost per hour $_____
   Total executive director expense $_____

Finance director
   Number of anticipated hours   _____
   Cost per hour $_____
   Total finance director expense $_____

Development director
   Number of anticipated hours   _____
   Cost per hour $_____
   Total development director expense $_____

Campaign manager
   Number of anticipated hours   _____
   Cost per hour $_____
   Total campaign manager expense $_____

Support staff #1
   Number of anticipated hours   _____
   Cost per hour $_____

Support staff #2
   Number of anticipated hours   _____
   Cost per hour $_____

Support staff #3
   Number of anticipated hours   _____
   Cost per hour $_____
   Total support staff expense $_____

Consultant #1
   Number of anticipated hours   _____
   Cost per hour $_____

Consultant #2
   Number of anticipated hours   _____
   Cost per hour $_____
   Total consultant expense $_____

Other (specify)
   Number of anticipated hours   _____
   Cost per hour $_____
   Total other expense $_____

TOTAL PERSONNEL EXPENSE $_____

EXHIBIT 5.2

Identifying Brochure Elements That Determine Cost

Brochure Image

Keep your constituencies in mind when you consider the program or service image the brochure should reflect. A small social service organization might warrant a simple two-color brochure, whereas a medium-sized art museum will demand greater attention to elements of design.

Who are your constituencies? _____

What type of image would speak to them all? _____

Information Presentation

How the story of what your organization will do with the funds raised by the major gifts campaign is told is almost as important as the telling itself. You are in a position to guide your constituencies' experience of this information. Put plenty of thought into it.

Will you use photographs? _____

How many? _____

Do you have the photographs in hand? _____

Will you use charts? _____

Will you use graphs? _____

Distribution

Considering how you will distribute your brochures will help you determine its size and appearance.

Will you mail your brochure? _____

Will it be self-mailing or require an envelope? _____

Will the envelope be business sized or will it have special dimensions? _____

Will the brochure be handed out? _____

At what types of events will it be distributed? _____

Quantity

To get an accurate determination of quantity, try to consider every potential use of your brochure. Don't assume that the total number of brochures needed equals the total number of prospects. Chances are you will need many more. How many will you need for each of the following groups?

Volunteers? _____

Staff? _____

Prospective donors? _____

Other (specify) _____

_____

Associate Help

What kind of assistance will you need to get your brochure completed? Consider this now so you can find the best fit for your needs and not have to scramble for help midway through the process; budget correctly.

Will you need a designer? _____

Will you need a photographer? _____

Will you need an illustrator? _____

Will you need a desktop publisher? _____

Drafting Your Budget

In Worksheet 5.1, you can begin drafting your own campaign budget, following the general pattern of the sample budget shown earlier. Your total expenses should be between 5 and 15 percent of the campaign goal. If they are significantly over that figure, review your projected expenses with the person most involved with managing your development department's budget. Your budget might be overestimating expenses or underestimating revenues. However, this result might also mean that your organization should reconsider conducting a major gifts campaign at this time.

Monitoring and Correcting Your Budget

An important step in budgeting is monitoring and, if necessary, correcting the budget. To do this, you need to see and approve invoices as they come in. If they do not normally come to your attention, arrange to see them as they are received. Compare them to the contracts and estimates you have. It is usually very helpful to add a column titled "Actual" to your final working budget so you can keep a running total of the final expenses.

When there is a variance between an estimate and the actual expense, it is time to take *corrective action*. This means discerning the cause of the variance, taking steps to help prevent it from happening again, and accommodating that variance elsewhere in the budget (if possible) by reducing an expense or by eliminating a line item all together. Variances are the reason the budget outline asked you to add in a 10 percent contingency amount.

Paying for Expenses

Campaign expenses are rolled into the campaign goal. If your organization's goal is $1,000,000 and likely expenses total $100,000, then you actually need to raise $1,100,000. Many people hesitate to include campaign expenses in the goal for fear prospects will "find out" and not want to give. Today most people are aware that it costs money to raise money and are not put off by campaigns that reflect this reality.

Sometimes organizations use the early gifts of board members and key campaign leaders as seed money to cover expenses. This is fine, but these gifts should still count toward the campaign goal.

This chapter illustrated how to put a budget together, why it is important to have a budget, and how you can monitor the budget as your campaign progresses. Remember, your campaign budget is a key management tool. Keeping on top of your budget is a way to avoid many problems and to increase the confidence of volunteers, who generally prefer supporting well-managed campaigns. In the next chapter you will learn more about volunteers.

WORKSHEET 5.1

Getting Started on Your Campaign Budget

First, write down the campaign goal determined in Chapter Three. Then fill out the budget outline below. Use the blank rows to add any other expense areas you have and their likely costs. Figure the percentage of your cost compared to your revenue by dividing total expenses by total income.

Campaign goal: _____

Income

Individuals	$_____	
Foundations	$_____	
Corporations	$_____	
Other	$_____	

TOTAL $_____

Expenses

Personnel

Executive director	$_____	
Development director	$_____	
Support staff	$_____	
Consultant(s): fund raising	$_____	
Other consultants	$_____	
Other staff	$_____	
_____	$_____	
_____	$_____	

TOTAL PERSONNEL $_____

Communications

Brochure	$_____	
Video	$_____	
Newsletters	$_____	
Web site	$_____	
Invitations	$_____	
Posters and signs	$_____	
_____	$_____	
_____	$_____	

TOTAL COMMUNICATIONS $_____

Research

Consultant	$_____	
Firm	$_____	

TOTAL RESEARCH $_____

WORKSHEET 5.1 (continued)

Special events	Admission-free cultivation	$_____
	Admission-free, large public kickoff	$_____
	Fund raising	$_____
	_____	$_____
	_____	$_____

TOTAL EVENTS $_____

Printing	Pledge cards	$_____
	Volunteer packets	$_____
	Photography	$_____
	_____	$_____
	_____	$_____

TOTAL PRINTING $_____

Donor stewardship and recognition	Donor plaques	$_____
	Tours	$_____
	Recognition events	$_____
	Hospitality	$_____
	_____	$_____
	_____	$_____

TOTAL STEWARDSHIP
AND RECOGNITION $_____

Volunteer management	Packets	$_____
	Training	$_____
	Hospitality	$_____
	Recognition	$_____
	_____	$_____
	_____	$_____

TOTAL VOLUNTEER
MANAGEMENT $_____

SUBTOTAL $_____

| Contingency @ 10% | | $_____ |

GRAND TOTAL $ _____
(_____ % of the
campaign goal)

CHAPTER 6

Identifying, Recruiting, and Training Volunteers

AN ACTIVE, INVOLVED volunteer force is one of the most important elements of your campaign. Volunteers are among your most likely campaign donors too. This chapter describes what your volunteers add to your effort, how to find them, and how to involve them.

Understanding the Importance of Volunteers

In Chapter One I emphasized that successful fund raising requires building relationships with people. Because *people give to people with causes,* major gifts fund raising can seldom be done in a mechanized way or without the involvement of enthusiastic, committed advocates. The most successful campaigns almost always involve some of the people who are naturally a nonprofit organization's most effective boosters and partners—its volunteers.

Literally everyone associated with your organization (volunteers, staff, donors, patrons, customers, and in many cases clients too) is like a walking billboard advertising the wonderful work your organization is doing. And many of your best prospects will be these people who are most intimately aware of your organization's many accomplishments, because they themselves are part of that success.

There has been significant debate for over a decade about the role of volunteers in major gifts fund raising and the degree to which campaigns can succeed without an adequate volunteer force to solicit gifts, especially in face-to-face meetings with prospective donors. You may be aware of successful major gifts campaigns that have been significantly staff driven. I have rarely seen them reach their potential, however. Organizations usually lack sufficient staff to cultivate and solicit the dozens and dozens of prospects whose gifts make these campaigns succeed. Moreover, members of an organization's staff are typically not as well connected to the prospective donors as its volunteers are.

And even after three decades in fund raising, I am still amazed by what happens to volunteers who participate in major gifts fund raising. They often become reinvolved, refreshed, and reinvigorated. When volunteers talk to people about their own values and why the cause is important to them and then hear the prospects speak from their own experiences and values, the volunteers' faith in the work they do is increased in very meaningful ways. Selling simply increases the enthusiasm of the salesforce. And enthusiasm is infectious.

Another important reason to involve volunteers in face-to-face solicitation is that when staff, especially senior staff, solicit, the prospective supporters may wonder whether they are really trying to raise their own salaries. Such concerns do not usually encourage people to give as they seldom see how this goal translates to meeting the program goals of the campaign.

It is also my philosophy that almost anyone can, to some degree, become an effective fund raiser. I have seen shy, reluctant volunteers, given proper training and encouragement, shine in campaigns. Even when they do not actually ask for the gift, they can speak from their hearts about why your organization is important to them. Accompanied by another volunteer or a member of the staff who is the designated solicitor, the shy but committed volunteers can become highly effective. You will be well served if you assist your volunteers to become strong ambassadors for the cause and mission about which they care deeply.

Think of it this way. You know your group can't afford big advertising campaigns. There's no money in the budget for full-page magazine ads or Super Bowl halftime commercials. But what you do have are those walking billboards, volunteers who are mobile advertisements for your missions. Just train them and support them so they feel confident about sharing their enthusiasm with others as they move through their lives.

Three Main Roles for Campaign Volunteers

Your organization's major gifts campaign will need volunteers to serve as campaign chairs, to serve as members of the campaign committee, and, possibly, to serve as honorary co-chairs. Here are sketches of those roles and brief job descriptions.

The Campaign Chair

Almost every campaign needs one or more chairs to provide top leadership and make the campaign visible in the community. These chairs must be people who command respect among the prospective donors and volunteers and who can speak eloquently about your organization's cause. They must also be donors to your major gifts campaign at a level that is significant and appropriate for their personal circumstances.

Campaign Chair Job Description

- Primary role and responsibility:
  - The primary role of the chair is to lead the fund raising efforts of the major gifts campaign.
- Timeframe: [month, year] to [month, year].
- Specific responsibilities:
  - Identify candidates for and assist in the recruitment of campaign volunteers.
  - Hold regular campaign committee meetings to review and direct the progress of the campaign and to ensure its success.
  - Maintain periodic contact with committee members to monitor and encourage their success.
  - Make a generous personal gift that will motivate and encourage others to give generously.
  - Assist in the identification of potential key donors.
  - Serve as a spokesperson on behalf of the campaign.
  - Permit your name and photo to be used in promotional material.
  - Attend major cultivation events.
  - Assist in the solicitation of key lead gifts.

The Honorary Co-Chairs

Honorary co-chairs may bring additional visibility to your campaign. Although honorary co-chairs are not expected to do the same significant work as chairs do, they must still support the campaign financially. Never use honorary chairs who do not support the effort financially.

Honorary Co-chair Job Description

- Primary role and responsibility:
  - The primary role of the honorary co-chairs is to validate and promote the campaign to the public.

- Timeframe: [month, year] to [month, year].
- Specific responsibilities of an honorary co-chair:
  - Permit your name and photo to be used in promotional material.
  - Make a generous personal gift to the campaign that will motivate and encourage others to give generously.
  - Attend major cultivation events.
  - Assist in the identification of key volunteers and potential donors.

The Campaign Cabinet, or Committee

The campaign cabinet, or committee, is the group of volunteer solicitors who are the campaign's workforce. Without this vital group, your campaign will seldom have a viable effort. You will see why if you review the gift chart you made in Chapter Three. Soliciting dozens and dozens of major gift prospects face-to-face would likely be impossible for your staff. Even if they did have the time, it is unlikely that they would have personal connections to all these prospects or enough influence with them to encourage their maximum participation.

Campaign Committee Member Job Description

- Primary role and responsibility:
  - The primary role of committee members is to work to ensure the goals of the campaign are met.
- Timeframe: [month, year] to [month, year].
- Specific responsibilities:
  - Implement the campaign plan with major responsibility for solicitations.
  - Make a leadership gift to the campaign that will motivate and encourage others to give generously.
  - Help plan solicitation strategies for top-level prospects, and personally solicit a select number of prospective donors.
  - Attend major campaign events.
  - Permit your name and photo to be used in promotional material.

Finding and Recruiting Volunteers

Volunteers who can work with staff on a major gifts campaign are typically found close to home, in the organization's inner circle that was discussed in Chapter Four. Look at the people you consider members of your organization's immediate family. Review your donor lists, member lists, audience members, and so on. They are already committed to your organization. They may become major gifts volunteers themselves or they may able to identify potential volunteers.

FINDING VOLUNTEER FUNDRAISERS

Look for volunteer fund raisers among

- Current board members
- Former board members
- Prospective board members
- Committee members
- Program volunteers
- Donors

- Participants
- Audience members
- Organization members
- Clients
- Families of clients
- Alumni

As a first step in finding volunteers and recruiting them to your campaign, make an informative list of prospective volunteers for your major gifts effort using Worksheet 6.1.

WORKSHEET 6.1

Identifying Prospective Volunteers

In the following chart, list as many prospective volunteer names as you can and indicate their current relationship to the organization (board member, donor, and so on), the person best positioned to recruit them, how important their involvement might be, and why they might want to volunteer (remember, the opportunity to help a cause one favors is a personal benefit).

Prospective Volunteer	Relationship to Organization	Who Should Recruit	Importance	Benefit to Volunteer
_____	_____	_____	_____	_____
_____	_____	_____	_____	_____
_____	_____	_____	_____	_____
_____	_____	_____	_____	_____
_____	_____	_____	_____	_____
_____	_____	_____	_____	_____

Volunteers are best recruited by their peers. No one is better able to sell something, whether it's a tangible thing or a cause, than someone who is already personally committed to it. This is logical, because we already know that the best person to solicit a gift is someone who has already made one. The same is true of volunteering. In addition, the volunteer recruiter is modeling behavior you hope the prospective volunteer will adopt.

The steps you take to recruit campaign volunteers will depend on these prospects' current relationship with your organization. If they are already program volunteers, then perhaps all another volunteer or a staff member needs to do is to take them out for lunch or coffee, tell them about the project and how it relates to what they are already doing with your organization, and describe how they will benefit personally from the new involvement.

People who are not yet involved with your organization may also be recruited. Ask members of your "inner circle" to help identify potential volunteers. Service clubs composed of local business leaders are excellent sources of names. Find someone who is already part of your "family" to help identify, cultivate, and recruit these people. Another good place to find new volunteers is among the citations in annual reports of other organizations whose campaigns have concluded. Reports almost always recognize key campaign volunteer leadership.

When you meet with the potential volunteer, mention the other volunteers already committed, the important role of the professionals, and the training and support offered to volunteers. Inexperienced fund raising volunteers almost always need this assurance before they decide to join a campaign committee.

MARKETING IS KEY TO VOLUNTEER RECRUITMENT

Don't talk just about how your organization needs volunteers. Talk about the ways the prospective volunteers' involvement might benefit them. Will they meet interesting people? Will they benefit from the increased capacity of the organization to meet its mission? Are the campaign's program and service goals things that they personally value?

Every volunteer who is participating in a fund raising campaign needs to receive a simple job description, as outlined earlier, explaining what is expected of campaign committee members, such as attending monthly meetings, participating in a certain number of cultivation events, reviewing prospect lists, and so on. This job description can be used as a recruitment tool, helping volunteers feel confident that they understand what they are being asked to do. You will also find that volunteers are more likely to sign on when the job description goes both ways. What will the organization do to help its volunteers succeed? The job description might tell volunteers they will be given accurate prospect research, clerical support, and training; become members of a team; be invited to cultivation events; and so on. Volunteer job descriptions help prevent the misunderstandings about roles and responsibilities that sometimes occur between organizations and their unpaid assistants. It is vital always to be honest and clear. If you expect a volunteer to plan and implement the cultivation events, say so. Volunteers, like everyone else, do not like making commitments and later finding out they didn't really know what was expected of them.

Training Volunteers

The purpose of volunteer training is to increase the confidence of your volunteers in order to increase their participation, to increase their ability to speak articulately about your cause and its campaign, and to increase their success. Confident volunteers feel more comfortable when they solicit their prospects. Volunteer training is one of the best investments you can make during a major gifts campaign. Confidence is best instilled through these methods:

Model the behavior. Make sure campaign leaders themselves have been trained and can set a good example. Make sure your recruiters have a positive attitude about the campaign.

Encourage informal training throughout the entire effort. Staff who work closely with the volunteers are in effect trainers. Staff should take advantage of every opportunity to remind volunteers of the campaign's purpose and how it answers the needs of the community and meets the organization's mission.

Make sure volunteers get answers to their questions. Volunteers should know whom to ask when they have questions. Encourage dialogue so they understand that asking questions is not an indication of weakness but an indication of commitment.

Bring in a professional trainer. Be prepared to have a consultant conduct a training session. Repeat the session as you recruit additional people throughout your effort. Also invite the trainer back to offer review courses as needed. The advantage to using an outside trainer is that volunteers, like most people, often pay more attention to what outsiders say, and so this special training will strongly reinforce what you are likely already telling them.

Here is a sample training agenda. (The material in the left-hand column can be handed out to participants as the session program.) Remember to leave time for questions and answers throughout the training.

SAMPLE TRAINING AGENDA		
	Who	**When**
Welcome and introductions	Campaign chair, Trainer	7:00
Review of agenda	Trainer	7:15
Overview of campaign goals	Campaign chair, campaign staff	7:20
Fund raising—what it means for our mission	Trainer	7:40
Translating features of the campaign's results into community benefits	Trainer, all	7:50
What it's all about—how fund raising happens—the Fund Raising Cycle	Trainer	8:15
Why volunteers are key to fund raising	Trainer	8:20
Past fund raising success stories	Campaign committee members	8:25
Key campaign strategies	Campaign chair, campaign staff	8:35
The volunteer tool kit	Campaign staff	8:40
Overcoming objections	Trainer	8:45
Role-plays	Trainer does one in front of room	8:50
Role-plays	Volunteers work in teams of twos	9:00
Sharing of role-play experiences	All	9:25
Next steps for the campaign committee	Campaign chair	9:40
Evaluation of training	Trainer, all	9:45
Adjournment		

The Only Thing Worse Than Training Volunteers Who Do Nothing

The only thing worse than training volunteers who ultimately do no solicitations for your campaign is neglecting to train the volunteers who do go out and do solicitations. Training pays off in increased confidence and commitment. It helps ensure that accurate messages about the campaign are disseminated. Training is almost always worth the expense.

A REAL-LIFE STORY OF THE POWER OF PEER TRAINING

A medium-sized environmental organization embarked on a $750,000 campaign with a very limited campaign budget. It was a member of a small alliance of environmental groups in its sparsely populated part of the country. Staff had no money to hire a trainer and were not sure if any existed in their area. So they called up other alliance members to ask if any of those groups' volunteers would meet with their own volunteers to talk about fund raising. A plain-talking, to-the-point volunteer showed up. He told the other volunteers, "You love your kids and want them to have a good life. Even better than yours. You want to leave them a legacy. Well, I'd like to leave each of mine a million bucks and then the same for the grandkids. But no-can-do. The bucks aren't in the bank. So I work hard for a better world. And that's why I fund raise for the environment. Instead of the big inheritance. Get it?" He then went on to lead a spirited discussion about some fund raising techniques he had learned over the past decade of preserving wilderness areas and open space in his state. They got it.

Supporting Volunteers with Volunteer Kits

Your volunteers want to be part of a team that is heading towards success. They need training, staff support and assistance, materials that are easy to access and use, and lots of encouragement and praise. Remember, they don't have to do this work. They are doing it because they care about your organization's cause. Good volunteers are worth their weight in gold!

The volunteer kit is one of the most useful campaign tools you can offer these vital assistants to your campaign. A kit can be a simple double-pocket folder containing a list of the volunteer's prospects with gift histories and contact information such as telephone numbers and addresses, brochures and other campaign promotional material, report-back forms, support documents (with titles like "Simple Answers to Hard Questions" and "Overcoming Objections"), a campaign roster with your name and number on it too, and any other aids you think appropriate.

Dealing With and Preventing Unproductive Volunteers

There is an adage in volunteer management that one-third of your volunteers will be enthusiastic in their work, one-third will be moderately productive, and one-third will not participate much at all.

You will naturally want to avoid telling volunteers they are no longer needed, as this can be unpleasant for everyone. Rarely will someone sign up for a campaign with the conscious intention of doing nothing. People almost always are well intentioned. So if a volunteer is not returning your phone calls or reporting in, you have several options. The first is to determine whether a personal situation is preventing the volunteer from participating. If that is the case, perhaps the volunteer can be more active at another time. It is important to be understanding when events the volunteer has no control over get in the way of campaign participation. When volunteers are simply not doing enough, it is sometimes best to just concentrate your efforts on others and spend more time with the people who are willing and able to be active.

When volunteers are disruptive or have a negative impact on others, however, you may have to remove them to protect other volunteers and the campaign. You should always strive to do this in a way that saves face for everyone involved. Your goal here is to encourage a graceful departure, not just to "get rid" of them. And there's another reason to remove inactive volunteers. If you let them stay, it can send a message to the others that it is OK to do nothing.

A REAL-LIFE STORY OF SMART VOLUNTEER MANAGEMENT

One medium-sized social service organization developed a clever way to deal with a major gifts campaign volunteer who was not very enthusiastic about the organization but who was, unfortunately, the campaign chair.

Because she kept complaining about the organization but was well connected to many key prospects, she was invited to chair the long-range planning committee, charged with dealing with some of the issues of concern to this volunteer.

Because she could not chair the campaign and the planning committee simultaneously due to the significant time commitments required by both positions, she had to step down as the campaign chair. Although this was not an ideal solution, it did respond to the needs of the organization.

Remember, if you hesitate to remove a volunteer, the welfare of the organization and its ability to meet its mission must take precedence over the needs or desires of its volunteers.

Sometimes, by the time you notice that some of your volunteers are inactive, the group's morale has already been hurt. Worksheet 6.2 will help you devise methods *now*, before your campaign starts, to keep up volunteers' energy and commitment. Don't wait. Do this now. Once you have completed it, show it to other staff to get their ideas. Refer to and act on this worksheet throughout the campaign. Put your ideas to good use!

The goal of this chapter was to give you critical information about one of the keys to your success—volunteers. I described where to find them, how to involve them, and how to train them. This understanding of the importance of volunteers' roles is a foundation for cultivating relationships with major donors, the topic of the next chapter.

WORKSHEET 6.2

Inspiring Your Volunteers to Be Effective

This chart lists the most likely reasons for volunteer participation and suggests some ways you can reinforce volunteers' motivations. After reading each reason and the typical ways to support it, describe some specific things you will do to support volunteers in their personal goals.

Why They're Here	Some Ways to Convey This	What We Will Do
To make a difference	Remind them the reason we're raising money is to meet community needs. Make sure they fully understand what a successful campaign can do for their community.	_____
To be part of something meaningful	Bring program staff or clients to campaign meetings to tell their stories firsthand. Try to relate each gift to what it will mean for the organization's program.	_____
To be part of a team	Volunteers are our natural partners. Make sure they know the organization can't do it alone.	_____
To be part of something successful	Tell them of past successful campaigns. Involve volunteers from those campaigns in the current effort. Incorporate some type of training in every meeting.	_____
To be appreciated	Recognize each volunteer every time there is a success, even if it wasn't exactly what we wanted.	_____
To be recognized	Show them their names in newsletters. Send them extra copies of press releases. Send them thank-you notes and mementos.	_____

CHAPTER 7

Cultivating Relationships with Major Donors

CULTIVATION IS A CONCEPT central to your entire fund raising program, not just to your major gifts campaign. As this chapter will demonstrate, successful cultivation of relationships with major donors can empower your volunteers and often means the difference between a token gift and a gift that represents a true investment in achieving your campaign's goals.

Defining Donor Cultivation

Donor cultivation is any activity that significantly deepens the understanding an individual has of a nonprofit organization's mission, programs, or goals. It is not a solicitation. Think of the word *cultivate*. Don't you imagine someone tending a garden? Carefully feeding and watering a plant over a long period of time? Cultivation is a *personal* action that seeks to nourish something so that it grows strong. That is what you do when you cultivate relationships with your prospects.

Cultivation precedes solicitation. Your prospective donors can benefit from cultivation in many ways, depending on the types of cultivation activities you offer. For example, they might have opportunities to learn more about your organization's program goals, ask questions, meet donors who are already committed, or meet key staff.

At the same time, *you also benefit*. While your prospects get to learn more about your organization, you get to learn more about them. What interests them? What are their questions and concerns about your program goals? Whom did they seem to enjoy speaking with the most?

Cultivation is key to relationship building and cannot be rushed. You should allow anywhere from two months to two years for a major gift to mature.

Understanding the Cultivation Connection— Your Bridge to Success

Think for a moment about a personal situation in your own life, a situation that required you to ask someone to do something for you. Perhaps you wanted to ask a neighbor to help you with a home repair. Maybe you needed a ride to work because your car broke down. Now think about the people you were most likely to ask to assist you. Were they total strangers or were they individuals you have gotten to know a little and feel comfortable with? Of course you would likely ask the latter, *because you have reason to believe they would say yes.* This is the key reason *involving your volunteers in cultivating prospective donors is central to the entire process of raising major gifts.* Volunteers get to know prospects and then feel more comfortable asking for their support. Remember, fund raising is about building relationships. It is hard to build relationships with people who meet your organization's key staff and volunteers only when they are being asked for money.

Cultivation is your chance to get to know prospects better, let them meet some of the organization's key people, hear and answer their questions about your goals, inform them about the important community needs your campaign is trying to address, and find out what programs, services, and plans appeal to them the most.

Ideally, your major gifts campaign will feature many different kinds of cultivation opportunities because prospects are not all alike—they respond differently to different interactions. Moreover, almost any contact, not only the ones you or others in the organization instigate, can become an opportunity for cultivation. You have to recognize these opportunities when they occur so that you may mold them into cultivating interactions. If a prospect comes to a reception honoring an outgoing board president or participates in a focus group or attends an informational briefing given by an expert in your field, that individual is demonstrating an interest in your field. This interest could be an excellent foundation on which to begin cultivating a relationship.

An easy way to tell if an interaction with a donor or prospect falls into the cultivation category is to ask these two questions:

- What does the prospect know *now* that she might not have known before? Is this important information about our organization?

- Was the interaction direct and face-to-face and personalized in some way? Did the volunteer or staff member involved speak personally with the individual? Was a letter or written communication personalized in some way?

If the answers to those questions are positive, then the interaction was probably cultivation.

Certainly you, other key staff, and your board members will probably instigate most of the cultivation activity. Meeting with prospects to update them on your programs or calling donors directly to thank them for gifts are just two good examples of successful cultivation. Send newsletters to your prospects, invite them to your parties, interview them for feasibility studies—keep them in your loop! You should cultivate relationships with all major donors and major donor prospects routinely, not just prior to or during a major gifts campaign. Remember, cultivation increases understanding about and interest in your organization, and understanding and interest increase people's confidence in the organization and stimulate their desire to support it. Indeed, for the most effective major gifts campaign, donors and prospects should be routinely informed about your organization *before* the campaign begins.

Of course not *all* contact will necessarily propel cultivation. Avoid simply sending generic letters to your prospects, especially those at the higher gift levels. Try to address them personally whenever possible.

COMMON TYPES OF MAJOR GIFTS PROSPECT CULTIVATION

More productive types of cultivation:

- Prospect comes to a reception honoring outgoing board president.

- Board member meets with prospect to give an update on programs.

- Board member calls donor to thank her for a gift.

- Prospect receives invitation to a selective party.

- Prospect is interviewed by a consultant for feasibility study.

- Prospect participates in a focus group.

- Prospect attends an informational briefing given by an expert in the organization's field.

Less productive or poor types of cultivation:

- Prospect receives a "dear friend" solicitation letter.

- Prospect receives a personalized solicitation letter.

- Prospect attends performance of an arts organization with no contact of the organization's representatives at the performance.

Who Cultivates Donor Relationships

Representatives of your organization who can speak about your mission, goals, and programs should be responsible for cultivation. Generally this includes senior administrative and program staff, board members, and campaign volunteers.

Think about sending someone to take a prospect out to lunch. Who are the people you would feel confident about asking to do this? Are they enthusiastic about the organization? Knowledgeable about current programs and future goals? Committed to the organization's future success? When volunteers cultivate relationships with prospects and donors, they are modeling behavior you would like those prospects and donors to ultimately enact themselves—that is, cultivating relationships with others interested in the organization.

Also, if volunteers who are ultimately going to be the solicitors are involved with cultivation, they will be more confident when the time comes to ask for a gift, because they will already have had opportunities to get to know their assigned prospects. However, most volunteers will not be able to handle the cultivation and solicitation of more than five or six major gifts prospects in any one year.

Common Objections to Cultivation

Here are some of the typical objections organization staff have to undertaking the cultivation process, and the answers to those objections.

We need the money now! Soliciting too early is like making a marriage proposal too early. The relationship usually needs to deepen before the prospect will be confident saying yes.

Cultivation takes too long! It is better to solicit a prospect successfully ten months from now than to solicit him unsuccessfully today.

Cultivation is too expensive! Cultivation events need not be costly. A cocktail party in the home of a volunteer, a hard-hat tour of a future facility, an informational briefing given by an outside expert about an important issue, a private meeting in the home or office of a prospect, a thank-a-thon are all examples of effective and low-cost cultivation activities.

We don't have anyone who can cultivate relationships with our prospects! If you don't have anyone who can take the time to cultivate, you are probably not ready for a major gifts effort. Instead, step back and review your inner circle of supporters to identify and recruit an expanded volunteer base. Remember, when cultivation includes face-to-face meetings on such topics as program updates, staff can often accompany volunteers. This may increase the confidence of your volunteers and their willingness to cultivate—and later solicit—prospects.

To begin the process of choosing the kinds of cultivation activities that will work best for your organization, try some brainstorming, using the guide on p. 75. Then use Worksheet 7.1 to create a list that will help you plan your campaign.

SOME COMMON CULTIVATION ACTIVITIES AND THEIR PROS AND CONS

Cultivation Activity	Pros	Cons	Cost	Comments
Private meeting in prospect's home	Probably the most effective—personal and confidential.	Busy people may be hard to schedule; volunteers *must* be well prepared.	Approximately 3 to 4 hours of staff time to plan, schedule, rehearse with volunteer, and evaluate.	Should be done with as many top prospects as possible; has great research possibilities; significantly increases volunteer's confidence in soliciting.
Small event with less than 50 guests	With the right speakers, a great way to spread enthusiasm; prospects see their peers participating; good way to groom volunteers and assess presentation skills.	Busy schedules can mean many are unable to attend; all presenters must be scripted and rehearsed.	Up to 25 hours or more of staff time to plan and coordinate; ideally volunteer host will pay for catering.	Gives inexperienced volunteers an opportunity to get their feet wet in a fairly risk-free way.
Feasibility study interviews conducted in the prospect's home or office by a consultant	Allows prospect to speak confidentially about the organization and its plans.	Must be part of a feasibility or planning study, which normally takes 3 to 4 months to complete.	$15,000 to $35,000 for 40 to 50 interviews.	

A REAL-LIFE STORY OF ACTING ON OPPORTUNITY

An environmental group with cash flow problems had considered canceling its annual open house. However, thinking of the bad image the last-minute cancellation might convey, staff went ahead with the event. At this open house, they met one of their donors for the first time and discovered his real passion was not in their new program on organic gardening, which was the focus of the major gifts campaign, but in their ongoing work empowering low-income communities to organize around the environmental issues most affecting them. Staff introduced the prospect to the organization's community organizer who, with the assistance of a campaign volunteer, later successfully solicited the prospect for a $5,000 gift. The donor became so involved with this project, he later gave a $25,000 gift to the organization's major gifts campaign. If staff had not provided an opportunity for this donor to meet them, it is unlikely they would ever have learned where his real interests lay.

WORKSHEET 7.1

Identifying Cultivation Opportunities

List every type of cultivation activity your organization might implement (get ideas from others too). Then list the pros and cons of each. As you do so, consider carefully what cultivation opportunities your prospects and donors are most likely to respond to.

Cultivation Opportunity Description	Who Would Be Responsible?	When Would It Happen?	How Much Would It Cost?
_____	_____	_____	_____
_____	_____	_____	_____
_____	_____	_____	_____
_____	_____	_____	_____
_____	_____	_____	_____

The Hardest Part—Getting Prospects to Attend

Have you ever put on a party and then wondered if anyone would show up? Prospective donors and your volunteers are busy people. All too often, staff and volunteers arranging an event spend too much time worrying about how it will look and not enough time on strategies to get people to attend. Here are some tips that may apply to your organization.

- Have volunteers call the prospects they know personally, *before* the invitations go out, in order to encourage prospects to read the invitations.

- Consider renting a van and giving people a ride to the event. Riding together can give them opportunities to get to know each other. Make sure a campaign representative rides along.

- Provide valet parking service if the event takes place in an area with limited parking.

- Make personal reminder calls the day before the event to encourage attendance.

WORKSHEET 7.1 (continued)

Whom Would We Invite?	Pros	Cons
_____	_____	_____
_____	_____	_____
_____	_____	_____
_____	_____	_____
_____	_____	_____

- Provide maps and directions, with a contact number in case people get lost.

- Feature a special guest people will want to meet—maybe a local celebrity who is sympathetic to your cause.

- Hold the event somewhere usually inaccessible to the public that people will want to see.

A REAL-LIFE STORY OF A SPECIAL OPPORTUNITY

An organization devoted to preserving local farms knew that most of its donors, although they appreciated rural life, were busy, affluent city people. The staff thought convenience would be important. So they used an upscale urban venue, the boardroom of a private bank, for a cultivation event, but the attendance was poor. Then they asked their volunteers to do a little "marketing research." The volunteers called the people who had been invited but did not attend and asked them where they would really like to go. Bingo! They wanted to see a real live farm and meet real live farmers. The resulting "Field Trip to the Family Farm" was hugely successful. As was the organization's campaign. This event is now an annual thank-you to major donors.

Here are examples of an invitation to a donor cultivation event and of a script for a telephone follow-up.

SAMPLE CULTIVATION EVENT INVITATION

Dear Mr. Roberto Leaton:

You have been an important part of our community's cultural scene, contributing to increased opportunities for adults and children alike to enjoy the performing arts. Thank you!

We believe that you might be interested in knowing about our small group whose purpose is to expand music education for low-income children and about our plans to expand our training program. We have seen some of our graduates go on to music careers as teachers, composers, and performers. One of our newest alumni, Lisa Smith, has just been accepted to the Juilliard School of Music.

We would like to invite you, along with a few others, to join us in sending Lisa off to music school and to meet our teachers who recognized and helped develop her talent. Please join us at:

River City Music Center
Tuesday, June 12, 2002, at 4:00 P.M.
123 Main Street

I will call you to see if you will be able to join us.

Thank you again.

Sincerely,

Harriet Goldberg
Campaign chair

SAMPLE SCRIPT FOR TELEPHONE FOLLOW-UP

Volunteer: Hello. Is Roberto there?

Roberto: Speaking.

Volunteer: Roberto, this is Harriet Goldberg. I'm on the service club's membership committee with you.

Roberto: Oh, yes. How are you?

Volunteer: Fine, thanks. I hope you're fine too. I'm wondering if you would have just a couple minutes to speak.

Roberto: Yes, now would be fine.

Volunteer: I may have mentioned that I'm on the campaign committee for the Music Center.

Roberto: Oh, I didn't know that.

Volunteer: Yes, it has been my passion for five years. In fact, two of my grandchildren learned music there.

Roberto: How nice!

Volunteer: Roberto, we are having a little gathering on June 12 to send one of our newest graduates off to Juilliard. And I was calling to let you know that I have just sent you an invitation to the event.

Roberto: That's very nice of you. I don't know if I can make it though.

Volunteer: I understand. I think you would enjoy the event and meeting some of our other volunteers.

Roberto: Well, thanks for telling me about it. I will look for the invitation in the mail.

Volunteer: Thanks, Roberto. Hope to see you there.

This chapter stressed the importance of cultivating relationships with major donors, a key concept in successful fund raising that empowers your volunteers and involves your prospects in your cause. Now that you have determined the cultivation events that should work best for your campaign, it's on to the heart of the major gifts campaign: solicitation.

Soliciting Major Gifts Prospects

IN THIS CHAPTER you will learn steps to take to make your solicitations successful.

Effective major gifts campaigns are actually a series of campaigns, beginning with the prospects believed most likely to make the largest gifts. Consult the gift chart you made earlier. Be sure to start soliciting people in the top level before you approach prospects in the lower levels. While you are working with the top tier, begin planning the solicitations in the next level, and so on. Then you can use early large gifts to raise the confidence and the sights of the people whose gifts you solicit later. However, as new prospects are identified throughout your campaign, they may be solicited "out of order."

Of course all volunteer and staff solicitors, whatever their gift levels, must be solicited for the campaign *before* they can begin to cultivate or solicit anyone else. They should not be put in the position of asking someone to do something they have not already done. You should be able to tell prospects that you have the staff and volunteer commitment they will likely want to see before they decide to give themselves.

Also remember that a match between the prospect's interests and the work of the organization leads to the most effective major gift solicitation. Prospects don't care about what the organization needs; they care about the ways the organization meets community needs. The return on the donor's investment is the community benefit that happens as a result of the work made possible by the donor's gift.

Assigning Prospects to Volunteer Solicitors

You will find it helpful to think not only of each major gift level but also of each major gift solicitation as a separate campaign. It has a separate financial goal, a unique prospect, one or more trained solicitors assigned to it, specific strategies set out for it, and a specific timeline.

The most important element in this campaign other than the prospect is the volunteer, or possibly staff, solicitor. But how do you decide which volunteer solicits which prospect? Solicitors are likely to be least successful when trying to secure face-to-face meetings with prospects they have never met. And people are more likely to give to people they know and respect. So you need to consider who has the best chance of success, that is, who is most likely to engage the prospect in a meaningful dialogue. The following list suggests four effective ways to match one or more solicitors to a prospect, beginning with the most effective and continuing in descending order.

First Ladder of Effectiveness for Assigning Solicitors to Prospects

- The solicitor is known and respected by the prospect and has given at the same level being asked of the prospect.

- The solicitor is known by the prospect and has given at a level that is equally meaningful. For example, a gift a gift of $5,000 may be as significant to the solicitor as a gift of $25,000 is to the prospect.

- The solicitor has been introduced to the prospect by a colleague or friend of the prospect who has helped with the cultivation.

- The solicitor has been involved in cultivating a relationship with the prospect.

Another ladder of effectiveness to consider has to do with organizational and campaign role. Again, the most effective solicitors are listed first.

Second Ladder of Effectiveness for Assigning Solicitors to Prospects

- The board president and the campaign chair
- The board president and the executive director
- The board president and the development director
- The campaign chair and the executive director

- The campaign chair and a campaign committee member

- A campaign committee member and the executive director

- A campaign committee member and the development director

- The board president alone

- The campaign chair alone

- A campaign committee member alone

- Any staff member alone

There are of course variables to consider in employing this ladder. Is the executive director well respected in the community? Effective in fund raising? Articulate? Is the board president shy and uncomfortable in fund raising? Comfort, capacity, and connections to the prospect are often more important than the titles. A volunteer who does not have a title in the organization but who is known by the prospect and has given at the same level being asked of the prospect is likely to be a more successful solicitor than the board president who does not know the prospect, for example.

At the top of the second ladder of effectiveness are seven suggestions for solicitation *teams*. A team is usually more effective than a single solicitor because two people have twice the talents and strengths of one. Moreover, knowing they can work with another person increases volunteers' willingness to make the calls. It's simply easier to do the job when you have help. And if one person "chokes" when it comes time to ask for a gift, the other is there to step in.

Although you may work with a consultant in some areas of your campaign, using a consultant as a solicitor is usually not the best approach because it makes your prospects think nobody connected with your organization cares enough to make the solicitation personally. However, it can work to your advantage if the consultant has relationships with your prospects, has been a part of your organization at an earlier time, or simply accompanies your volunteer solicitors as a supporter. It is almost never advisable to have your consultant make a solicitation alone. Always have a volunteer or member of the staff as part of the team.

Now begin charting your own course for effective solicitations by matching solicitors and prospects using Worksheet 8.1. Make special note of the number of assignments you give to each volunteer. Unrealistic expectations can limit volunteers' enthusiasm and success. As mentioned earlier, do not expect a volunteer to be responsible for cultivating and soliciting more than five or six prospects a year.

WORKSHEET 8.1

Matching Solicitors to Prospects

List your top prospects and assign a solicitor or, preferably, a team of solicitors to each. Assign a backup team too. Note the amount of the gift to be requested and any points solicitors should make that are likely to be important to that particular prospect.

Prospect	Ask Amount	Solicitor Team	Backup Team	Important Points to Make
_____	_____	_____	_____	_____
		_____	_____	_____
		_____	_____	_____
_____	_____	_____	_____	_____
		_____	_____	_____
		_____	_____	_____
_____	_____	_____	_____	_____
		_____	_____	_____
		_____	_____	_____

Testing Prospect Readiness

You may wonder how you can determine whether a prospect is ready to be solicited. Ask yourself these questions:

- Do I know what the level of this person's interest is in the campaign, if any? How certain am I?

- Do the campaign's program and service goals match this person's known interests and values?

- Has this person met the campaign leaders? The organization's leaders? Has this person been given an opportunity to participate in a meaningful dialogue? How certain am I?

- Have this person's questions been answered to the person's satisfaction by me or someone else in the organization? How certain am I?

If you can answer yes confidently to all these questions, you are likely ready to solicit the prospect for a gift.

Finalizing Prospect Information

At this point the campaign manager or an assistant can produce an updated and final form of the prospect information sheet for each prospect so you and your solicitors can use the information in planning your solicitation strategies. Note that it is absolutely essential that this form remain confidential. Never show it to your prospects.

UPDATED PROSPECT INFORMATION SHEET—CONFIDENTIAL

Use these headings for your prospect information sheet:

Prospect name(s)
Address (home and office)
Phone
Fax
E-mail
Occupation
Title
Employer
Employer address
Source of income (earned and unearned)
Prospect's interests
Spouse/partner
Spouse/partner's interests
Children/family

Giving history to our organization
Giving history to other organizations
Other involvement with our organization
     (volunteering, subscribing)
Community activities
Names of people connected to us who are
     connected to this prospect
Why we think the prospect is interested in our cause
Best team for cultivation
When should cultivation take place
How should it take place
Best team for solicitation
Strategies for solicitation
Gift range for our campaign
Sources of information for this sheet
Date sheet was filled out
Name of person filling out sheet

Arranging Appointment Logistics

Often just getting the appointment to meet with the prospect is the hardest part of the solicitation. When trying to get prospects to agree to meet with solicitors, remember to make sure that the prospect has attended at least one cultivation event and has previously met at least one of the solicitors asking for an appointment now. Here's a sample script that suggests some strategies for talking with the prospect about a meeting.

Usually the best place for the appointment is where the prospective donor feels comfortable and the meeting will not be interrupted. The prospect's home or office is often a good choice. Try to avoid restaurants or other public places. You don't want the waiter to stop by with the coffeepot just as you are asking for the gift.

SAMPLE SCRIPT FOR REQUESTING AN APPOINTMENT

Prospect: Hello

Solicitor: Hello, is Jane Corelli there?

Prospect: This is Jane.

Solicitor: Jane, this is Bob Khamishon. I'm a volunteer with the campaign to expand our library collection. I met you last week at Herman Samuels' house where we announced our new plans. Would now be a good time to speak for a few minutes?

Prospect: Yes, although I am really busy.

Solicitor: Oh, I totally understand how busy you must be. I only need a few minutes of your time right now. What did you think of our new plans?

Prospect: Well, I didn't really get to stay long. It was so crowded!

Solicitor: Yes, we were so pleased at the number of our friends who wanted to be there. I'm calling to ask if Sarah O'Connor, our campaign chair, and I might meet with you to discuss our project.

Prospect: You're not going to ask me for money are you? I hate that! How can you stand to fund raise? Isn't it awful?

Solicitor: Well, yes, I am going to ask you to do exactly what Sarah and I have done—make an investment in our community. And I must admit fund raising does not come naturally for me. Sometimes I feel uncomfortable. But this project is so important to me that I am willing to ask people to support it to make it

happen. I can't say I'm a pro at it. I just believe in our mission. Maybe after we meet, you could tell me how I've done?

Prospect: I don't have a lot of money right now with my boys away in college.

Solicitor: Yes, I remember your telling me how much they liked to read. Our expanded collection will include lots of books for young people. And our donors can make pledges now and pay their gifts over time. We even accept credit cards.

Prospect: OK, so how much are you going to hit me up for? Just ask now and get it over with.

Solicitor: Well, I'd rather wait until we meet to go into any details. I really want to go over our plans and give you some information first. Because of your past support, I really think you will be excited about what this campaign is going to enable us to do for our community.

Prospect: Well, I could meet next Wednesday at 2:00 in my office. But I only can give you twenty minutes.

Solicitor: Jane, that would be wonderful. I know how busy you are. Wednesday at 2:00 in your office at 345 Main Street, Suite 678. Let me give you my number in case you need to change the time. It's 456-7890. Thanks so much! See you next week. [*Bob calls Jane to confirm the day before the appointment.*]

Some people like to be solicited with their significant others and some do not. If you are not sure whether to suggest including a spouse or partner in the meeting, ask the prospect's preference. Just make sure you get the names correct (this information should be on the prospect information form). Married couples do not always have the same last name. And sometimes unmarried couples do. The important thing is to be sure that all the decision makers in the family hear about the campaign goals.

A REAL-LIFE STORY OF A WIDOW AND A BROKER

A small, independent school wanted to solicit an alumna from the Class of 1946 for the lead gift to a campaign to renovate the chemistry lab. Knowing that the prospect's husband was deceased, the development director was concerned about her comfort in making financial decisions without him. They also believed that her financial adviser's recommendation had been part of her decision to make an earlier gift. So they invited the adviser to the meeting. The development director knew right away that the prospect was really interested in the campaign. She had loved science when she was a student there and had been especially fond of her chemistry teacher, Dr. Watson. In fact, her most recent gift was to support a scholarship in his memory. But when the development director asked for the gift, the prospect seemed shocked. Was the amount too high? Did she object to being asked by the development director? She just said she would think it over. Months went by. The development director felt she had failed because the prospect did not return her calls. But she continued to keep the adviser informed of the campaign as it progressed, encouraging him to let the prospect know how things were going. Finally several months later, the prospect called out of the blue to say she would make the gift. She went on to say how much she resented her "husband's financial adviser" trying to influence her every move. That is why she waited to tell the school, to make him understand it was her decision to make and not his. The development director never invited the adviser to join them again.

Finally, even though face-to-face solicitations are almost always the most effective, there are other ways to ask for support. Sometimes you or your solicitors will not be able to get an appointment. Perhaps the prospect will insist on making a commitment on the phone. This is fine! Thank the person for the support. Some people want to give but for various, largely personal reasons do not like to meet. Some people may never answer their phone, using a message machine to screen their calls instead. When you encounter this situation, be sure to leave a detailed message. For example, a solicitor might say: "Hello, Mrs. Montoya. This is Mary Jensen. I am a volunteer with the Animal Shelter's fund raising campaign. I know you love companion animals, and I think you will like to know what our plans are. I will try to call you again later this week. If you would like to contact me, my number is 234-5678. Thank you." If the prospect never returns your calls, then follow up with a letter.

Developing a Script

Once you have determined the team of solicitors for each prospect, it is important to develop the strategies for each solicitation. You need to know how to capture the attention of each prospect. What areas is the prospect most interested in? What aspects of the organization's programs appeal the most? It is important to emphasize how the major gifts campaign fits into the organization's strategic plan and how the gifts received will enable the organization to meet its mission. Remember, your solicitors are your salesforce. They are selling intangible products (community improvements, community benefits, and the like) to potential investors. They need to know the product inside out, and they must be prepared to talk about it effectively.

Volunteers may initially balk at the idea of using scripts to solicit their prospects. However, a script is an excellent tool for working out and rehearsing strategies that the volunteers can then use with more proficiency in the face-to-face meeting at which they will ask for a specific amount of money. Make it clear to volunteers that they do not read from the script at the meeting anymore than an actor reads from a script during a performance. However, rehearsing with a written script can greatly increase their comfort level with their task.

The script should contain the main points the team wants to make, describe who says what and who makes the ask, and identify the amount the donor will be asked to give. It will cover the essentials but be much briefer than the actual conversation. In the following sample script, the development director, Dave; the campaign chair, Charmaine; and a prospect who has never given to the organization before, Wendy Chen, are meeting in Ms. Chen's home.

The most important thing to do after you ask your prospect for a specific amount is to remain quiet until the prospect responds. As solicitors rehearse the script, they can practice saying, "I'd like you to consider a $25,000 gift. What do you think?" Then they should watch the second hand on a clock. How many seconds pass before they begin to feel uncomfortable? They should practice until they can wait comfortably at least sixty seconds. And they shouldn't forget to breathe.

Also consider the approach of a successful volunteer solicitor who works with small social change organizations and who has a script format she says has rarely failed her. She begins each solicitation by telling the prospect: "My colleague and I are here to do three things: to update you on our work, to tell you why we are involved ourselves, and to ask you to join us in helping change the world." She observes that by making these points early on in the meeting, the "cat is out of the bag" and everybody can relax.

Work with your solicitors to develop a script for each solicitation. Use the following list of topics as a starting point.

The introductions and thanks

A brief statement of the purpose of the appointment

A brief summary of the organization's mission, history, recent successes

A description of the campaign goals, both program and financial

SAMPLE SOLICITATION SCRIPT

Charmaine: Ms. Chen, thank you so much for allowing Dave and me to meet with you today. We know you are busy so we will try to be brief. [*Takes a moment to describe mission and goals.*] Our center has been turning away low-income clients for the past two years because we do not have the funds to underwrite the fees for everyone who needs our help. We believe that if we raise $1 million for an endowment fund, we will be able to expand our client base and serve at least three hundred more people every year. I am the campaign chair, and I have made a commitment that is one of the biggest I have ever made. Dave has given also.

Wendy: Yes, I have heard of your fine work. [*All three chat for several minutes about the mission and the community need. Dave and Charmaine answer Ms. Chen's questions.*]

Charmaine: Ms. Chen, we know you have been very generous in supporting community needs. In fact, you are viewed as one of our area's philanthropic leaders. People respect you. We believe that your support can encourage others to do the same. That is why we would like you to be our lead donor and make a gift of $100,000. [*Dave and Charmaine remain silent for thirty seconds.*]

Wendy: Hmmm. I'm interested in your work. Let me think a moment. [*Dave and Charmaine remain silent for sixty seconds.*]

Wendy: I have a few questions. How will the endowment actually work? Do you understand investments?

Dave: We have a small cash reserve fund now that has been invested conservatively and has produced about 5 percent each year in income, which we generally reinvest. So we have a good track record handling investments. This new endowment would also be invested, but we would spend about 3 percent of the income to underwrite client fees. We could then serve three hundred more children and adults. The other 2 percent of the income from the investments would be reinvested. This is the way we will increase the actual amount in the fund.

Wendy: I understand. May I think about this and get back to you?

Charmaine: Of course. We would like to leave this information about our campaign with you. I would like to call you next week. Would that be convenient?

Wendy: Yes.

Dave: Ms. Chen, thank you so much for your time. It has been our pleasure seeing you.

A discussion of how these goals contribute to meeting the mission and producing specific community benefits

The request for a gift (specific)

WAIT PATIENTLY FOR RESPONSE; LISTEN CAREFULLY

Questions and answers

The prospect's decision

The next steps

Thank you!!

If there is more than one solicitor, they need to decide which topics each one will address. They also need to develop questions to ask the prospect. For example, they might ask what the prospect thinks of a recent organizational accomplishment and how the prospect feels about the campaign's program goals. During the scripting process, always remember that solicitors should foster a conversation with the prospect, not deliver a lecture. A good way to ensure this is to ask the prospect open-ended questions throughout the meeting.

Asking for a Specific Amount

Volunteers may wonder why they are told to ask for a specific amount. When organizations don't know much about their prospects, they may hope these prospects will somehow know the ideal amount to give. Prospects are often generous but never psychic. It is best to ask for a specific amount. For example, you might ask for $5,000, telling the prospect that you have secured a lead gift of $100,000 and are also looking for a number of important gifts in the $5,000 to $10,000 range. Such specifics give prospects an idea of how you see their participation in your campaign. They let the prospects know how important their gifts are. When you leave the amounts up to the prospects, they may think their gifts aren't very meaningful to the effort.

Overcoming Prospect Objections

One of the greatest fears of volunteer solicitors is that they will not know how to answer prospects' objections. In the sample script given earlier, did you notice how Bob, the solicitor calling to set an appointment, dealt effectively with some of the prospect's objections? Read the following tips and then reread the script looking closely at the ways Bob used his volunteer training to good effect. Worksheet 8.2 will help you deal with objections.

- When the prospect complains about the time involved, make sure she knows you heard her. If possible, reassure her ("I'll only take a few minutes").

- When the prospect criticizes something about the organization, acknowledge the concern and, if possible, turn it into a positive. (Bob turned the crowded party into a successful turnout.)

- When the prospect tries to rush the process and proceed directly to the solicitation, tell him you aren't prepared to ask for a gift just yet. If he insists on making a commitment over the phone, thank him!

- When the prospect mentions financial problems, mention options for giving ("We accept pledges and credit cards").

- When the prospect makes negative comments about fund raising, take this opportunity to let her know how committed you are. She will want you to be real, not slick.

In addition, remember these general tips:

- When the prospect asks a question you can't answer, it is all right to say you don't know. Offer to find the answer and then get back to him.

- When the prospect says the requested amount is too high, it is all right to ask her what amount would work for her.

- When faced with any objection, remember that objections indicate interest in the organization. If the prospects weren't interested, they probably wouldn't have agreed to meet with you in the first place.

Getting Beyond Fear

Here are some common fears voiced by volunteers about soliciting prospects and some ways to deal with those fears.

I can't be too assertive. They'll think I'm pushy. Often being assertive is seen as a sign of commitment.

I will have to know everything there is to know about my organization. Relax. You're a human being, not an encyclopedia. It's OK to admit you don't know. Promise you will find out and then get back to the prospect with the answer.

They'll criticize my organization. Sometimes criticism is an indication of interest.

They will be able to tell I'm nervous. My hands will shake! Being nervous is all right. Turn it into a positive: "I'm a little nervous, because I'm so committed to this project!"

WORKSHEET 8.2

Anticipating Objections

List all the objections to supporting your campaign you can think of and then draft some good responses. Share this list with others to develop more ideas. Use the final set of questions and responses in your volunteer trainings.

Objection   **Response**

_____   _____

_____   _____

_____   _____

_____   _____

_____   _____

_____   _____

_____   _____

_____   _____

_____   _____

_____   _____

They won't have enough money to make the gift I ask for. Make sure they know about pledging to pay over time or using credit cards. Generally people who really have no capacity to give will not want to embarrass themselves by agreeing to meet in the first place.

They'll reject me. Even if someone does say no, it won't be a personal rejection. And no often means "not now." Find out what has led to the decision. Ask if you might contact the prospect again later in the campaign.

I'm not as wealthy as they are. It would be ideal if you could make exactly the same size gift. But your gift may be just as meaningful to you. Consider saying something like, "This is one of the biggest gifts I have ever made."

I will be too scared to make the ask. Rehearse. Take someone with you. Also, tell prospects right away what you are there to do. Make sure you have identified yourself on the phone or in letters as "a member of the campaign committee." Always make sure they know you are there to talk about their supporting your campaign. Never lie to a prospect to get the appointment.

I will fail and let my organization down. The only way to guarantee failure is not to try at all. Even if prospects do not support your campaign financially, they have met you and learned more about the important work your organization is doing.

A REAL-LIFE STORY OF CONQUERING FEAR

A volunteer who has dedicated more than thirty-five years to fund raising for various causes says the best way she can prepare for a solicitation is to write down her worst fears beforehand. She claims it helps her stay grounded and not make mountains out of molehills. In all her years of asking people for money, none of her worst fears has ever happened!

Increasing Your Comfort Level

To increase your own and your solicitors' comfort level with solicitation, script and rehearse the meeting as described earlier. Practice. Practice. Practice. Make sure you discuss with the other person on your team who will say what and who will actually ask for the gift.

Rehearse various ways of phrasing the ask that make the donor's importance clear, such as, "We are hoping for five donors in the $15,000 range and that you will be one of them; people respect you, and your support at the $2,500 level will mean a lot to our success."

Take materials with you. Take notes of information you are afraid you might forget. Take the volunteer's tool kit, described in Chapter Six, with information about the prospective donor, campaign literature, and answers to frequently asked questions.

Reviewing What to Say During the Appointment

There are many suggestions in the chapter for conducting a successful solicitation. Because this is such an important part of the major gifts campaign, here's a review of the highlights for meeting with prospects.

Thank them for meeting with you and for their past support if any. Introduce your colleague if necessary. Briefly state what your organization's campaign is all about. Remember money is the means, not the end. Stress how a successful campaign will benefit the community and how many people will be served. Connect these benefits to what you know about the prospect's own interests and values.

Tell them how their money will be used. Tell them why you are committed to the campaign and that you have made your own financial gift. But remember that you are not there to give an oration. It is a conversation. The prospects must be given opportunities to speak too. This is often the *only* way to learn what they are thinking.

When you have covered these areas, and you have given the prospects time to ask questions, you may be ready to ask for the gift.

Be direct and look right at them.

Be proud. You are doing something wonderful for your community.

After you ask for a specific amount, stop talking! Try not to begin speaking again, even if the silence is uncomfortable.

Listen to their response carefully. Of course yes is the answer you want. But work with what they say. Answer all their questions. Be respectful and assertive. Remember, no often means "not now."

Repeat their decision. ("I understand you want me to send you our financial report." "I understand you want to think about it and I will call you back next week." "I understand you want to make a pledge of $500 now and then consider another $500 after we have raised more money.") Thank them no matter what the outcome is!

For more information about major gift solicitation, refer to the excellent and easy-to-read *Getting Major Gifts* (Klein, 1999). I recommend buying a copy for each of your volunteers. Get at least one copy for your office.

In this chapter, you have learned how to prepare for solicitations, how to get the appointment, what to do at the appointment, and how to deal with objections. You are now ready to learn about monitoring all these activities as part of your overall major gifts campaign.

CHAPTER 9

Monitoring Your Campaign

CAREFUL MONITORING allows you to identify problems and create workable solutions so you can succeed in reaching your campaign goal. This chapter guides you in tracking the progress of your campaign from beginning to end and in using what you learn to manage campaign strategies and encourage volunteers and staff.

Holding Campaign Committee Meetings

Information sharing is critical to a major gifts effort. Most campaigns will want to have at least three campaign committee meetings—an initial meeting or kick-off at which volunteers have a chance to meet the organization's key leaders and each other, a reporting meeting at which the organization recognizes those volunteers who are especially effective, and a victory meeting at the campaign's close to celebrate success, to encourage the completion of any outstanding solicitations, and to recognize all the volunteers. Ideally these meetings will be attended by as many campaign leaders as possible—including honorary chairs and working chairs—plus the board president. Depending on the length of your campaign, you may want to hold meetings more frequently, perhaps monthly.

A great deal of information can be shared at these meetings, as this sample campaign meeting agenda illustrates. However many meetings you hold, it will be essential to maintain regular contact with all your volunteers to ensure that they complete their assignments in a timely fashion.

SAMPLE CAMPAIGN MEETING AGENDA	
Welcome and introductions	Challenges
The gift chart—what we have secured, what remains to be secured	Upcoming cultivation events
	Volunteer needs
Report from program staff	Review of solicitation techniques
New prospects—information gathering	Next steps
Assignment of new prospects	Next meeting
Success stories	Adjournment

Managing Ongoing Reporting

In the ongoing reporting and information sharing among staff and volunteers outside the campaign meetings, information must flow in both directions. The staff must inform solicitors of pledge forms and gifts that come in and of campaign results in general. The volunteer solicitors must return report-back forms to staff in a timely manner. These forms are vital to maintaining detailed information on pledge fulfillment; the data they contain can prove invaluable in not only this but also your next campaign.

There are several ways to ensure that volunteers get the information they need in a timely manner. When volunteers are on-line, staff can easily disseminate weekly or even daily campaign bulletins to them. Be sure these campaign updates credit the volunteers who have successfully solicited gifts. You can also update volunteers by fax, phone, and regular mail. Including campaign stories in your regular newsletters is helpful but they must not take the place of the more immediate volunteer updates.

Report-back forms are one of the most valuable tools in campaign management and evaluation. After every interaction the campaign volunteers have with a prospect, they should fill out simple report forms and return them to your office either by fax, e-mail, or mail. The information on these forms is then entered into the computerized database or other files that your campaign maintains on prospects and donors. It can then be analyzed and used to adjust the ask, change the solicitation team, alter planned strategies, and more.

It is often difficult to get volunteers to return the report-back forms. They get busy and often they fail to see the forms' importance. However, it is essential to go to some lengths to get them returned as they are an impor-

---

SAMPLE REPORT–BACK FORM

Confidential Form
Please fax back to Rosa Jackson, (123) 456–7890
Or mail to her at 123 Main Street, Your City

Name of prospect:

Name(s) of volunteer(s):

Type of interaction:

Date of interaction:

Summary of discussion:

New information:

Needs of volunteer:

Volunteer's planned next steps:

Prospect's planned next steps:

Changes to file information (address, phone, and so on):

Form filled out by:

Date form filled out:

---

tant record of prospect interactions and are often the best source of vital information about the campaign's prospective donors. Even if a prospect does not respond to your campaign with a gift, information about the solicitation may be extremely helpful in the future. To improve return rates, try these techniques:

- Staple a self-addressed, stamped envelope to each form.
- Tell your volunteers why this information is critical and how it will help them today and other volunteers tomorrow.
- Make it fun. Give awards for returning forms in a timely manner. Recruit a member of the campaign committee to serve as the "report form czar."
- Be sure your name, address, and fax number are on each form in case the envelope gets lost. Try typing your fax number in large print at the top along with a reminder.

A REAL-LIFE STORY OF A REPORT FORM CZAR

A medical research institute was undertaking its first big major gifts campaign in over two decades. When the new development director started working there just one year before the campaign launch, she discovered the donor records were kept on index cards in the proverbial shoe box. To make matters worse, most of the information was very old and incorrect. As the campaign progressed slowly but surely, she realized how critical the new information on those report-back forms was. But her busy volunteers just weren't returning them. So she thought about what kind of reward she could offer to encourage a better response. Because they were affluent, flowers and candy wouldn't do. Then a light went on! What did her volunteers really want? They wanted parking passes for the normally physician-only parking garage. Parking was a limited resource in their congested urban setting. So each month she awarded a one-week pass to the volunteer who returned the most forms. By the time the campaign closed, not quite at goal but close, her records showed that 87 percent of the forms had been returned.

Evaluating the Campaign

To maximize the benefit of every campaign, the evaluation process must be ongoing. If you need to employ alternative strategies, it will have to be done during the campaign. If you wait until the end to evaluate, it will be too late to change course. So keep key leaders informed throughout the campaign. Be optimistic but realistic with volunteers at all times.

Once the campaign is complete, write a report stating what you have learned, what worked, what didn't, what you would do differently the next time, and so on. Compile this report as soon after the campaign closes as possible. This final evaluation will be an invaluable tool in planning your next major gifts effort.

Jump-Starting a Stalled Campaign

Your ongoing evaluation and monitoring may reveal that your campaign, just like your car on occasion, is getting sluggish, slowing down, or even coming to a complete halt. The best way to deal with these problems is to prevent them from happening in the first place.

- Make sure you have enough gas (volunteers and qualified prospects) and it is the right octane for your kind of campaign.

- Make sure your road map is accurate and easy to read.

- Make sure the route you have selected is the best one.

- Make sure your timeline is appropriate. Driving long distances at a fast speed without stopping can be hard on your engine.

- Take plenty of rest stops to review your roadmap in evaluation sessions. They're good for your engine—and for the drivers.

- Make sure your bags (volunteer tool kits and scripts) are packed, and you haven't forgotten anything.

- Be sure every driver has his or her own map.

- Be a good driving instructor and enjoy the journey!

If you think your campaign has become stalled, the first thing to do is to make sure it is in fact stalled. Campaigns, again just like cars, cannot always move at the same speed. You may be crawling through traffic now, but that doesn't mean you will never reach the journey's end.

Characteristics of a stalled campaign may include dwindling attendance at campaign meetings; having few prospects left to solicit, no further cultivation events planned, or no solicitations taking place even though you still have a way to go to reach the campaign goal; a poor response rate to your phone calls; and a frequently absent campaign chair. However, because you are bound to run into some of these characteristics from time to time, they do not necessarily mean your campaign is stalled. It may just be going through a temporary slowdown.

To get through a slowdown or to get restarted after a stall, you must take some corrective steps.

First, ask your volunteers how they are feeling about the campaign. Be open and candid. Listen carefully to what they say. Also work on improving communication about goals and achievements. Make sure you are communicating frequently and regularly. Try to put everyone involved on a listserve. Have program staff or clients who will benefit from the campaign's goals attend meetings and share their stories with volunteers. Bring in volunteers from other organizations that have conducted successful campaigns and ask them to talk about their achievements. Recognize volunteers' successes, however limited, and remind them how the campaign will help the organization meet its mission.

Bring in a trainer for a refresher course for your volunteers. Examine your scheduling. It might be appropriate to change the time, place, and location of campaign meetings, for example.

Consider new leadership. Identify additional prospective donors. Identify more campaign committee members who can be solicitors.

Consider bringing in a campaign consultant to help you strategize next steps on an alternate course.

Finally, consider whether it's time to take a break and reassess your goals and timeline.

Worksheet 9.1 will help you monitor your campaign with an eye toward preventing stalls.

WORKSHEET 9.1

Preventing Campaign Stalls

Complete this chart now, and then reassess each element periodically during the campaign to see whether you need to address it. For example, if you think the number of remaining prospects has become too low for achieving your goal, try to involve your new donors in identifying additional prospects. If you are concerned about having enough volunteers, your new donors may help you there too by joining the campaign committee themselves or identifying others interested in your organization's cause.

Element of Success	How It Relates to Our Campaign Specifically	Current Assessment of This Element	What Can Be Done to Improve the Situation	Who Must Be Involved in the Improvement
Realistic goal: what it is, who determined it	_____	_____	_____	_____
Demonstrated need	_____	_____	_____	_____
Adequate numbers of qualified prospects	_____	_____	_____	_____
Committed campaign chair(s)	_____	_____	_____	_____
Adequate numbers of enthusiastic volunteers	_____	_____	_____	_____
Personal gifts in hand from all leaders	_____	_____	_____	_____
Adequate campaign management and volunteer support staff	_____	_____	_____	_____

WORKSHEET 9.1 (continued)				
Element of Success	How It Relates to Our Campaign Specifically	Current Assessment of This Element	What Can Be Done to Improve the Situation	Who Must Be Involved in the Improvement
Gift acknowledgment and reporting systems in place	_____	_____	_____	_____
Adequate training for staff and volunteers	_____	_____	_____	_____
Adequate opportunities for cultivation	_____	_____	_____	_____
Realistic timeline and plan in place	_____	_____	_____	_____
Communication plans in place	_____	_____	_____	_____
Stewardship and recognition plan in place	_____	_____	_____	_____

Taking Action When the Gifts Don't Come In

Every major gifts fund raiser's secret fear is that the prospects won't give. Here are some things to check if too few prospects are responding positively to solicitations for major gifts.

- Is the case for the campaign expressed succinctly and persuasively?

- Are the prospects properly qualified and rated? In other words, are you sure they have the ability to make the gifts, a belief in your cause, and a connection to your organization through their interests or through another person?

- Are your prospects adequately cultivated before they are solicited?
- Are your volunteers well trained and assigned to the appropriate prospects?
- Are your volunteers actually *asking* for the gifts?

Although adjusting your goal downward is not an ideal step, it is not necessarily fatal. If gifts are coming in more slowly than you had anticipated and you cannot correct the cause of this result, you might consider phasing the campaign. For example, if your goal is to raise $1,500,000 over twelve months and you come to believe $1,000,000 is more realistic, you might consider your present campaign to be the first phase of an effort that will run eighteen months. To keep your volunteers involved and motivated, you must communicate this new information to them as soon as the decision is made and tell them why the decision makes sense for the organization's ultimate success.

COMMON REASONS CAMPAIGNS FAIL

- They do not have enough qualified, rated, and connected prospects (the number one reason).
- Solicitations are not preceded by sufficient cultivation.
- Volunteers are failing to actually *ask* for the gifts.
- The goal is unrealistic (it reflects an internal need, not a fund raising reality).
- Volunteers are not well supported by the staff.
- Staff are doing most of the solicitations because there aren't enough volunteers.
- The community need the campaign addresses is not well articulated or is not real.

Celebrating Your Success

When monitoring and evaluation tell you the campaign has met its goal, it is important to have a special event to celebrate that success. It might be a simple reception for donors and volunteers at your organization's facility or an elaborate affair in a hired ballroom. Whatever you do, remember that the goal is to recognize your donors and volunteers. They are worth their weight in gold. Treat them accordingly!

In this chapter you got started on monitoring your campaign and began to establish a system for identifying potential problems and thinking of ways to solve them. You also learned how to jump-start a stalled campaign. The next step is to create a calendar that can guide you, your staff, and your volunteers throughout the entire major gifts effort.

CHAPTER 10

Staying on Track

A CAMPAIGN CALENDAR is an essential tool in a successful major gifts campaign. This chapter illustrates how to put the major elements of the campaign into a calendar format, with clear indications of who does what, when, and how. This calendar builds confidence in your volunteers, assures them there is an end in sight, helps you and others pace the work and meet important deadlines, keeps everyone on track, and even serves as a journal that will help you prepare for your next effort.

Understanding the Campaign Calendar

A campaign calendar is, like the gift chart, a useful management tool. It helps you monitor and evaluate the timeliness of your work and avoid potential disasters. It outlines a future-oriented plan, but it is not written in cement. You can adjust activities and their due dates as necessary. After the campaign, you can compare your original campaign timeline to the final version of your calendar that shows when things really happened and learn practical lessons that will guide you in the development of your next campaign plan.

As when you are creating any calendar of events, your dates should be conservative estimates not unrealistic goals. Err on the side of allowing more time than you need rather than on the side of setting extremely optimistic deadlines. Remember, a common complaint among fund raising volunteers is that the organization has unrealistic expectations! Be good to yourself and others, and let reality be your guide.

One way to use your calendar is to review it at the end of each week, going over all your recent accomplishments and making to-do lists for the next week. Highlight areas of concern. Although primarily used by your campaign manager and campaign staff, it can serve as a guide for other staff and your volunteers. It is almost always for in-house use only.

Selecting What Goes into the Calendar

Your calendar should contain realistic completion dates for major objectives and for the key tasks necessary to complete those objectives. Imagine that for some reason a new person has to manage your campaign without you or your staff. What would that individual need to know to successfully implement your major gifts campaign? It is this key information that you include in your calendar.

A simple way to proceed is to list all your major objectives along with their key tasks without putting in any dates. Then add the completion date for each objective. Working backward, add realistic dates for completing each task. A good way to start your list of objectives is to review all the areas covered in the first nine chapters of this book.

It's good to remember that many of your major objectives and their tasks will overlap. For example, while you are identifying your top prospective leaders, you might also be developing your campaign case. Therefore your calendar will not be in strict chronological order.

In the following example of a campaign calendar, be sure to notice the benchmarks. Benchmarks are important accomplishments in your campaign. If the campaign does not achieve a particular benchmark on time, that is a red flag. Pay attention to it, and take corrective action. For example, if your board does not give its formal approval to the program and fund raising goals of your campaign at any early stage in the planning, the campaign could face serious problems later when you solicit every board member for the campaign or request permission to hire campaign staff. Share your concerns about any unmet benchmarks with your supervisor or campaign chair immediately.

Creating Your Campaign Calendar

Now create your own campaign calendar using Worksheet 10.1 on page 114. You might plan on distributing copies of this calendar to your volunteers at your first campaign committee meeting. As the campaign progresses, it is sometimes useful to distribute updates so volunteers know exactly what the campaign has achieved so far and what it still has to accomplish—and therefore what they have accomplished and what is still expected of them. Of course monitoring this timeline is almost always the responsibility of your organization's staff. You want your volunteers to devote their time to cultivating relationships with and soliciting the prospects!

SAMPLE CAMPAIGN CALENDAR

Activity	Who	When	Comment
1. Campaign overview			
Determine community need	Staff		
Compare with strategic plan	Staff		Involve chair of board planning committee
Create or expand program plan	Staff		Take to board program committee
Determine program budget	Staff, board finance committee		
BENCHMARK: final approval of program plan and budget	Board of directors		Review with key board members before final vote
2. Campaign materials			
Create case expression for campaign	Staff		Involve chair of board public relations (PR) committee
Determine ideal campaign materials	Staff		
Develop materials budget	Staff		
Finalize types of material	Staff		
Create promotional materials, volunteer kits	Staff		Involve PR committee
BENCHMARK: complete key materials			
3. Prospecting and rating			
Review donor base to create initial prospect list	Staff		
Review initial list and rate prospects	Board development committee, board		
Meet with key leaders to expand prospect list	Volunteers, staff		

SAMPLE CAMPAIGN CALENDAR (continued)

Activity	Who	When	Comment
Rate new prospects	Volunteers, staff		Ongoing throughout campaign as new names are suggested
Determine research activities	Staff		
BENCHMARK: finalize initial prospect list			List will expand as new names are identified throughout campaign
Hire research consultant	Staff		
4. Gift chart and dollar goal setting			
Create gift chart from prospect list to date	Staff		
Set initial campaign goal	Staff		
BENCHMARK: approve initial campaign goal	Board of directors		
5. Identify, recruit, train volunteers			
Review current and former volunteer list	Development committee, staff		
Create initial campaign volunteer list	Staff		
Identify prospective campaign chairs	Staff, development committee		
Determine cultivation and recruitment plans	Development committee, staff		
BENCHMARK: cultivate and recruit campaign chairs	Board of directors		
Review initial campaign volunteer list with new campaign chairs	Staff		

SAMPLE CAMPAIGN CALENDAR (continued)

Activity	Who	When	Comment
Expand campaign volunteer list	Campaign chairs		
Assign prospective volunteers to current volunteers for cultivation and recruitment	Development committee, staff		
BENCHMARK: cultivate, recruit campaign volunteers	Volunteers, staff		
Conduct campaign training and fund raising review	Consultant		
Solicit all campaign volunteers and board of directors	Board of directors, campaign chairs		Must have financial support from 100%
Solicit key staff	Executive director		
BENCHMARK: all "family" members are committed to give			

6. Assign prospects

Activity	Who	When	Comment
Review prospect list	Campaign volunteers, staff		
Determine connections, solicitation strategies	Campaign volunteers, staff		
Assign prospects to volunteer teams	Campaign volunteers, staff		Ongoing throughout campaign

7. Cultivation

Activity	Who	When	Comment
Determine cultivation opportunities	Staff, campaign volunteers		
Schedule cultivation events	Staff		
Implement cultivation events	Staff		Ongoing throughout campaign as necessary
Invite prospects	Staff, campaign volunteers		

SAMPLE CAMPAIGN CALENDAR (continued)

Activity	Who	When	Comment
Attend cultivation events	Campaign volunteers, prospects, staff, board of directors		
8. Solicitation			
Solicit top-level prospects	Campaign chairs, campaign committee, board, staff		Fill in gift chart as pledges come in; adjust goal as necessary
Begin planning for second-level solicitations			
BENCHMARK: finish top level			
Begin second level			
Begin planning for third-level solicitations			
BENCHMARK: finish second level			
Begin third-level solicitations			
Begin planning fourth-level solicitations			
BENCHMARK: finish third level			
Begin fourth level			
Begin planning fifth-level (final) solicitations			
Finish fourth level			
Begin fifth level			
BENCHMARK: finish fifth level			

SAMPLE CAMPAIGN CALENDAR (continued)

Activity	Who	When	Comment
9. **Monitoring and evaluation**	Staff	Ongoing throughout campaign	Regular reports to full board are essential
Prepare regular and final campaign reports	Staff		Very useful in planning future campaigns
10. **BENCHMARK: announce campaign close and victory**	Campaign chairs, board, staff		Communicate with all donors
Recognize donors and volunteers	Board, campaign chairs, staff		
11. **Stewardship**			
Plan proper fiscal management of all funds raised	Board finance committee, board, staff		Stewardship is a vital part of your entire development program.
Communicate program progress to donors and volunteers	Staff, board		
Plan and implement ongoing stewardship program	Staff, board, volunteers		

WORKSHEET 10.1

Creating a Campaign Calendar

Complete the columns in this campaign calendar, using the sample as a guide. Remember to include benchmarks. Use extra sheets of paper as necessary. Review the worksheets you have already created and the earlier chapters for guidance.

Activity	Who	When	Comment
_____	_____	_____	_____
_____	_____	_____	_____
_____	_____	_____	_____
_____	_____	_____	_____
_____	_____	_____	_____
_____	_____	_____	_____
_____	_____	_____	_____
_____	_____	_____	_____
_____	_____	_____	_____
_____	_____	_____	_____
_____	_____	_____	_____
_____	_____	_____	_____
_____	_____	_____	_____
_____	_____	_____	_____

In this chapter you began creating a calendar that will help you keep your major gifts campaign on track so it can achieve its goals. Now you're ready to move on to learning about stewardship, one of the most rewarding and important concepts in deepening relationships with your donors.

CHAPTER 11

Providing Stewardship for Major Donors and Their Gifts

IN THIS CHAPTER you will learn what stewardship means, how it can deepen your relationships with your donors, and strengthen your overall development program.

Defining Stewardship

Stewardship is an attitude that should permeate your entire development program. It is what you do with your donors from the moment they make the gift and onward. It includes acknowledgment, recognition, involvement, and communication. It shows how your organization feels about your donors. They are not checkbooks. They are people who care passionately about your campaign case and deeply about your organization's success. You will find that if your treatment of them equals their passion about your mission, your entire organization will benefit.

Think of it this way. You and your donor are entering into a relationship. You have been cultivating the relationship, and at some point the person said yes. When the person made the gift, this deepened the relationship even more. It is like getting married. There is cultivation (courtship), a proposal (the solicitation), and a commitment ceremony (the gift). But the relationship does not end there. This is really only the beginning! Don't walk away from the relationship just because the check has arrived. (For more information about this important subject, read the well-written and interesting *Beyond Fund Raising,* Grace, 1997.)

However you thank your donors, stewardship is vital to your organization's future. Remember, everyone connected with your organization is a walking billboard for your organization. Make sure your campaign leaders thank, thank, and thank again the volunteers and donors who make

A REAL-LIFE STORY OF EFFECTIVE STEWARDSHIP

A national scientific research organization that concentrated on cutting-edge science had a limited development budget and donors spread over the entire country. The development director was at a loss as to how to provide proper stewardship for these donors beyond the perfunctory thank-you letter and occasional newsletter. He called ten of his donors to ask them to offer suggestions. Although they appreciated the timely acknowledgments, they told him the one thing they really wanted was information about the scientific research. Could he possibly mail them some summaries of some of the more interesting studies? He immediately spoke with their research director, who began to create summaries especially for nonscientists. The results were astounding. Within a year a study group of donors was founded 2,000 miles from the organization's office, with two more groups planned for elsewhere in the country. The research director began to visit the study groups each year to meet the donors and give stimulating talks. Five years later the organization had fourteen study groups around the country, many in nonurban areas of such states as Iowa, North Dakota, and Wyoming. Giving from donors in the study groups increased three times more than giving from other donors did. One of the study group donors, an estate planning attorney, has now begun a planned giving committee for the organization to perpetuate the research long into the future.

financial and program success possible. Simple recognition is often the most meaningful—personal letters, ads in local papers listing all donors' names, plaques in the organization's lobby.

It is also important to continue to communicate with your donors after the campaign closes. Tell them how their funds are being used. How is the community benefiting? Whose lives are being changed as a result of their gifts? When they understand the difference their gifts have made, they will be interested in continuing to invest in your mission.

Be sure to plan stewardship activities that are appropriate for each donor. People often feel uncomfortable if they think a nonprofit organization is spending too much money on them in relation to their gift. The tangible stewardship of $100 donors should be different from the tangible stewardship of major donors who give $10,000.

Here are some ways to communicate with donors after the campaign.

- Acknowledgment letters thanking them for their gifts

- Letters describing how the community has benefited from their gifts

- Regular newsletters with client successes and program stories

- Annual reports with audited financial statements

- Calls from volunteers reporting on the successful use of donors' gifts

- Thank-a-thons in which volunteers call only to thank and update donors

- Tours

- Invitations to admission-free events

- Opportunities to meet nationally known individuals involved with your organization's cause

- Informal presentations in a comfortable venue by experts, perhaps reporting on new research or recent events relating to your organization's cause, especially from a national or international perspective

---

SAMPLE ACKNOWLEDGMENT LETTER

Dear Mr. Martin:

Thank you for your most recent gift of $1,000. It is always nice to hear from someone who has been part of the Center's family for such a long time.

Over the past several years, your gifts, totaling $17,350, have enabled us to help many families find permanent housing and leave life on the streets. Your generosity and compassion have meant so much to them and their children. On their behalf, please accept our most sincere gratitude.

We are hopeful you will be able to come to our 25th Anniversary Party on September 15, from 3:00 to 6:00 P.M. You will be receiving an invitation shortly. In the meantime, we are enclosing a copy of a crayon drawing by one of the children whose family has recently moved into a clean and bright three-bedroom house.

Thank you again for making such a tremendous difference in the lives of so many.

Sincerely,

George Quintera
Executive Director

SAMPLE INVITATION TO A DONOR BRIEFING

Compassion-creates-giving-creates-action-creates-solutions

Everything you do affects everyone and everything. We are all connected.

To honor your generous giving, we are pleased to invite you to meet international expert Dr. Amelia Brown and hear about the ways our work influences international efforts on four continents. Please join us on July 8, from 2:00 to 4:00, in the executive board room of the Bank of Commerce, 123 Main Street, Our City. RSVP: (123) 456-7890.

Shouldering the Responsibility for Stewardship

Stewardship is a joint responsibility of the staff, board, and other key volunteers. The finance chair must ensure proper fund management practices are in place, and the executive director must ensure that programs are properly planned and implemented. The development director or executive director should work with the board or other volunteers to plan and implement the stewardship program. Being involved with stewardship increases volunteers' appreciation of the difference your organization makes to the community. Meeting and thanking donors, whether through thank-a-thons or in person, can be deeply meaningful to volunteers, whose commitment deepens as they communicate the organization's valuable work to others.

Depending on the size of your organization's board, it may want to consider instituting a stewardship planning committee or task force. This group should work with staff to develop ideas for the organization's stewardship program for different levels and groups of donors. Board members' involvement in this process will also increase the likelihood that they will be supportive of budgeting for stewardship.

To gain an overview of what your organization is currently doing to demonstrate its stewardship of its donors, complete Worksheet 11.1 with the help of others, as instructed. Then use the completed worksheet to develop next year's budget and plan your stewardship program.

WORKSHEET 11.1

Planning for Stewardship

Complete the middle column of this worksheet and then enlist key fund raising staff and volunteers (for example, the board development committee) to help you fill in the third column by brainstorming ideas for the future. Use the blanks in the first column for additional stewardship activities.

Stewardship Activities	What We Do Now and How	Additional Efforts
Acknowledge gifts in a personal way as appropriate to the donor	_____	_____
Prepare mementos that relate to our mission	_____	_____

WORKSHEET 11.1 (continued)

Stewardship Activities	What We Do Now and How	Additional Efforts
Provide updates and other communications, newsletters, and reports	_____	_____
Make personal calls to report on successes	_____	_____
Conduct thank-a-thons	_____	_____
Offer tours	_____	_____
Provide insider information about our cause	_____	_____
Introduce donors to program people who are close to the mission	_____	_____
Continue stewardship even if giving slows	_____	_____
_____	_____	_____
_____	_____	_____

Congratulations! You have now created a successful beginning to your major gifts campaign. Celebrate your successes throughout your effort, and take pride in making your community a better place in which to live.

Useful Publications

Bancel, M. *Preparing Your Capital Campaign.* San Francisco: Jossey-Bass, 2000.

Bennis, W. *On Becoming a Leader.* Reading, Mass.: Addison-Wesley, 1992.

Broce, T. E. *Fund Raising: The Guide to Raising Money from Private Sources.* (2nd ed.) Norman: University of Oklahoma Press, 1986.

Bryson, J. M., and Alston, F. K. *Creating and Implementing Your Strategic Plan.* San Francisco: Jossey-Bass, 1996.

Burlingame, D. F. (ed.). *Developing Major Gifts.* New Directions for Philanthropic Fundraising, no. 16. San Francisco: Jossey-Bass, 1997.

De Pree, M. *Leading Without Power.* San Francisco: Jossey-Bass, 1997.

De Pree, M. *Leadership Is an Art.* New York: Dell, 1989.

Grace, K. S. *Beyond Fund Raising.* New York: Wiley, 1997.

Grace, K. S., and Wendroff, A. L. *High Impact Philanthropy.* New York: Wiley, 2001.

Howe, F. *The Board Member's Guide to Fund Raising: What Every Trustee Needs to Know About Fund Raising.* San Francisco: Jossey-Bass, 1991.

Klein, K. *Getting Major Gifts.* (3rd ed.) Oakland, Calif.: Chardon Press, 1999.

Mixer, J. R. *Principles of Professional Fundraising: Useful Foundations for Successful Practice.* San Francisco: Jossey-Bass, 1993.

Muir, R., and May, J. *Developing an Effective Major Gift Program: From Managing Staff to Soliciting Gifts.* Washington, D.C.: Council for Advancement and Support of Education, 1994.

Prince, R. A., and File, K. M. *The Seven Faces of Philanthropy: A New Approach to Cultivating Major Donors.* San Francisco: Jossey-Bass, 2002.

Rosenberg, C., Jr. *Wealthy and Wise: How You and America Can Get the Most Out of Your Giving.* Boston: Little Brown, 1994.

Rosso, H. A., and Associates. *Achieving Excellence in Fund Raising: A Comprehensive Guide to Principles, Strategies, and Methods.* San Francisco: Jossey-Bass, 1991.

Rosso, H. A. *Rosso on Fund Raising: Lessons from a Master's Lifetime Experience.* San Francisco: Jossey-Bass, 1998.

Seiler, T. L. *Developing Your Case for Support.* San Francisco: Jossey-Bass, 2001.

Seltzer, M. *Securing Your Organization's Future: A Complete Guide to Fundraising Strategies.* New York: The Foundation Center, 1987.

Strand, D. J., and Hurt, S. (eds.). *Prospect Research: A How-to Guide.* Washington, D.C.: Council for the Advancement and Support of Education, 1986.

Wacht, R. F. *Financial Management in Nonprofit Organizations.* (2nd ed.) Atlanta: Georgia State University Business Press, 1991.

Warwick, M. *The Five Strategies for Fundraising Success: A Mission-Based Guide to Achieving Your Goals.* San Francisco: Jossey-Bass, 1994.

Notes

Lightning Source UK Ltd.
Milton Keynes UK
UKOW07f1318220916

283555UK00002B/16/P